Light From An Eclipse

Light From An Eclipse

Nancy Lagomarsino

The Marie Alexander Poetry Series, Volume 8
Series Editor: Robert Alexander

White Pine Press • Buffalo, New York

Grateful acknowledgment is made to the editors of the following publications, in which some of the material in this book previously appeared: *Key Satch(el)*, *The Prose Poem: An International Journal*, *The Prose Poem 1992*.

Publication of this book was made possible by support from Robert Alexander and with public funds from the New York State Council on the Arts, a State Agency.

First Edition

Printed and bound in the United States of America

Library of Congress Control Number: 2005920855

Cover photograph: "Eclipse Sequence Over Africa,"
        ©2001 by Fred Espenak, www.MrEclipse.com

ISBN: 1-893996-32-8

White Pine Press
P.O. Box 236
Buffalo, New York 14201
www.whitepine.org

To Mother
with a wink and a smile

Be ahead of all parting, as though it already were
behind you, like the winter that has just gone by.
　　　　　　　　　　　　　—Rainer Maria Rilke

Beauty and the beast, and you're the beauty.
　　　　　　　　　　　　　　　—Dad

the first snow settles
like a bed sheet onto grass
in time falling harder
blanketing the forgetful gardener's rake
a wooden box of horseshoes
until even gravestones seem part of nature
the oldest tilted back
and the path is deep and everywhere

*A*lzheimer's disease, the country my father approaches, has its own sky and shore. We watch helplessly, as he drifts away in a rowboat without oars. How is his new country different? The same kitchen, the same backyard, yet untethered. I have become a walking memory, waiting to be forgotten. The other day, when I called to say that I'd be coming for a visit, Mother put him on the phone, and he boomed, "Nancy! I recognize your voice!"

Watching a video we made of their fiftieth wedding anniversary party last year, I realize how little he participates, though we didn't notice then. Instead of listening to people, he waits for them to stop talking so that he can contribute his next remark, masking his mild disorientation with jovial laughter. He's never been the kind of man who would sit around with his wife and daughters just chatting or arguing about abortion. In order to spend time with Dad, you need to do something with him, like swimming, a walk, or getting the hibachi ready for a cookout. When we were kids, our family moved a lot. He'd put up a swing on a good tree, build a standing sandbox, install a basketball hoop, croquet course, badminton net, climbing bar. I asked Mother when she first realized something serious was wrong. She said it was when they took the car to get the brakes fixed, and the next day he had no memory of doing that.

I'm not even tempted to try to sort out the moments in search of a significant one. Maybe it was the time he started to drive the car away, while I was still climbing into the back seat, or the time he insisted on steering the canoe under the bridge at high tide, nearly knocking off my head. With so many stones on the beach, how can I choose the one that came first?

*M*other explains that Alzheimer's disease exaggerates a person's traits. A normally chatty person might become obsessively talkative, a quiet person introverted and silent. Dad's sociability has gone into overdrive. If anyone strays near, I grow tense, fearful that he'll start in on how smart and capable his three daughters are.

At eighty, he has more energy than a toddler who doesn't nap. While some of us slumber after lunch, he busies himself in the basement. I find him on the floor putting together an old plastic puzzle of the United States, checking the picture on the front of the box for clues. He's wearing sneakers, khakis, and a plaid shirt. Not for long, though, since he changes his clothes several times a day. "Why does he do that?" I ask Mother, during one of our hushed chats. She sighs. "Oh, it gives him something to do."

He beats me regularly at horseshoes, always gracious in victory. Standing well back, he tosses his horseshoe in a graceful arc through the air and around the pin. "You haven't had a chance to practice," he reassures me. He practices every day, in a civil war with himself, the gray horseshoes against the blue. Gray usually wins. We don't know why that is.

On every walk around the block, he points at one particular weathered cape and says loudly, "They're not married!" Pointing may sound like a small thing, but it gets to you. At the beach, his long arm shoots out, as he identifies with relish a woman in a skirted bathing suit fifteen feet away. I remember as a child pointing at the few constellations I knew and naming them. Dad's constellations are in his neighborhood—a house, a woman, each a star linked invisibly to another star.

Oct. 9, '92

Dear Nancy,

When I first started out to write about the history of my own life and the cities and towns I used to live in it was a lot of fun & I enjoyed digging into the past to remind myself who lived where and when. Lately, however, it has become something of a bore and I find myself getting a little tired of the whole business!

I'm going to use a different approach this time. The heck with detail and no more wondering where so and so lived, who graduated from High School, or when did Andrea (just an example) move from Southboro to Bow, N.H. I haven't started my new approach as yet but I wanted you to understand why my approach is different.

Enough of that! I decided to stop out of the church choir. It's not that I didn't enjoy singing but I noticed that my heart was beating faster and I seemed sort of nervous. You'll remember that a little while ago I had a problem with my blood pressure. I decided that it was because I was a bit nervous as a new-comer. So that's behind me. I wrote a short note to our choir director and explained this to her. Incidentally she is a terrific director and as attractive as can be. She also has a good sense of humor!

Can you ever imagine a lady in her 70s climbing out a window onto the porch roof just to scrape a little paint off the glass! That's nothing compared to climbing an extension ladder to paint a bit of house trim! Your Mother amazes me some time.

Your anniversary card came in the mail yesterday and it was very thoughtful of you. I hate to admit it but we have been so busy with this and that that we entirely forgot!

Much love to all. It will be so nice to share Thanksgiving with you!

Dad ♡

*T*he minute I arrive, bleary from the four-hour drive from our house in New Hampshire to Cape Cod, Dad invites me to the basement to show me his office. Standing before a sepia photograph, he points and says, "You may not know who all these people are," so I bite my lip and listen, while he identifies my grandparents, aunts, and uncles to me. This past summer he spent hours typing his autobiography down here in the coolness, but he'd forget how his old manual worked, and eventually his tinkering broke it. In fact, he's gone through three typewriters lately, including the Historical Society's electric typewriter Mother borrowed to type the minutes.

When he asks Mother to make copies of the autobiography at a Xerox place, so that he can mail them out, she stalls. "It needs some revision," she tells him tactfully. His accustomed modesty has been overridden by a need to remind himself and others of his accomplishments, as in a list of eighteen "HONORS RECEIVED." Among them:

2.   *When I was a member of the Student Body at Springfield College I was elected member of the College Student Council.*

7.   *I was chosen out of my Battalion to attend the School for Personnel Services at Washington & Lee University at Lexington, Virginia.*

9.   *I was chosen by many schools to give their Commencement address. Boston English High School gave me an award for the many talks I gave before the entire Student Body. (The award was a volley ball which I still have.)*

14.   *I was given a special award for "being a leader in education throughout New England."*

16.   *Over 10 applicants I was chosen Capt. of the Life Guards at*
        Old Orchard Beach.

On another sheet, titled "PASTORATES HELD BY MY FATHER," he
writes,

> EAST BOSTON. *Around the corner of the Church was a YMCA. As*
> *time went on I was fortunate to get a part-time job setting up pins in*
> *the bowling alleys. That was a long time before they had developed an*
> *automatic device. Across the street from our house was a Baptist*
> *Church which had the unusual custom of haveing a speaking contest. I*
> *was lucky to get first place for telling how George Washington actually*
> *cut down a Cherry Tree!*

These reminiscences, cut to the size of the typing and stuffed in
old manila envelopes, take on the authority of museum exhibits. I
imagine Dad as a pilot on the order of Orville or Wilbur Wright,
lifting off in a glider constructed entirely from sheets of autobi-
ography.

Dad thinks he's humoring Mother when he agrees to register with the Dementia Study at the Veterans Hospital in Bedford, nearly two hours away. "There's nothing wrong with my memory," he tells the doctor and recites, *'Twas brillig, and the slithy toves/Did gyre and gimble in the wabe,* from the poem "Jabberwocky" by Lewis Carroll. He insists he's never felt better in his life and offers to do the frogstand, that is, to crouch and put all his weight on his hands, a holdover from his college gymnastics days. The doctor announces that Dad will have to stop driving. His words are: "I order you to stop driving." In his deepest voice, Dad replies, "Sir, I've never had an accident in my life!"

The doctor asks Mother what's been hardest about all this for her. Talking this way in front of Dad is too much for me. I jump up and invite him for a walk on the grounds, more like a campus than a hospital. Dad holds a doctorate in education and has spent most of his professional life on campuses. Now, circling only one brick building, he feels lost.

What's hardest for Mother, she tells me later, is that they can't talk things over anymore. Though Dad sits through movies and TV shows with her, he can't discuss them. In the supermarket, she finds herself envying a couple debating which canned soup to buy.

Beyond the shadow of the ship,
I watched the water-snakes:
They moved in tracks of shining white,
And when they reared, the elfish light
Fell off in hoary flakes.
　　　　　—The Rime of the Ancient Mariner

Newly married, Dad joined the Heritage Club and filled the bookshelves with authors such as Dickens, Mark Twain, and Coleridge, in illustrated editions meant to be passed from one generation to another. Thumbing through their pages transports me directly to childhood, when words took up space between the enchanting pictures. Dad still loves to read, though it's hard to tell how much he absorbs. So much pleasure can be found in the ritual of settling down with a book and finding friendship, however brief. "I'm through with this," he announces after an hour, returning a thick library book to the pile. Presented with my Father's Day card, he scans the message like a speed-reader, laughs heartily, and puts it on the mantel. The front depicts a night sky filled with constellations. On the inside, I wrote, *To the Biggest Star in the Sky.*

I'm not sure when he stopped, but Dad used to compose verse and poetic prose, as in "FRIDAY—THE FINAL DAY OF 1982," a faded account typed on onionskin and entombed under plastic in an album:

> *... there were the breakers of our Atlantic Ocean rolling at high tide upon the clear sands of Nauset Beach. A beautiful sight with a high sea, product of the Moon's eclipse, tossing its waves high upon the beach.*
>
> *We strolled as close to the sparkling water as we dared and marveled at the miniature geysers which spouted, some three to*

five inches high, over the sands left bare by retreating waves. Some breathing of shell fish, underground air pockets, who is to say? I dug with my hands, admittedly fearing a cut from some sea shell, but uncovered nothing.

Inspired by his commemorative impulse, I churned out rhymes at an early age, and in second grade I completed a novel in pencil titled "RICKY." Dad took my pages to work and turned them into a typewritten book in a black binder. On the inside front cover, I glued a square of paper and wrote in my best penmanship, *Dedicated To My Father.* Chapters include "Pretty Banged Up," "Fire!," and "Saved Or Not," portraying the adventures of an active boy named Johnny Briggan, who rescues a wolf cub from a forest fire. Eleven chapters in ten pages, later revised for a fifth-grade English assignment—demonstrations of my lifelong respect for economy of effort. If I were able to go back and do it over, I'd make Johnny a girl.

Worries about Mother and Dad pursue me through a crowd of goldenrod and into pinewoods, where the sound of the brook relaxes my eyes, allowing me to gaze outward. I come here often, seeking the silence water imposes when it takes on a voice. Across the ravine, lichen-covered boulders hold themselves still, as though departing glaciers told them to wait. It feels strange to be so involved with my parents again, after decades of comfortable distance.

When I woke from the dream that is childhood and went into the world, I carried the dream with me—you might say I've treated my childhood like a favorite shirt worn every day. How could I leave my childhood in a drawer? For so long, it was my only garment. Photographs show me gliding along with my family, but inwardly I was reliving one of those vivid dreams we remember more easily than the day and night that surround it. Today, I balance on a stone that rises above the brook, close to my parents, yet removed. Caught in the current, a small branch hurtles past like a child on a bicycle.

I offer to drive the round-trip to the Veterans Hospital for the second of Dad's appointments, but Mother relegates me to the back seat on the way up. Near Plymouth, clouds turn to hard rain, and the windshield fogs. I reach from the rear to try to work an inadequate defroster. Massive semis pass us and cut in front, drenching any hope of visibility. A green exit sign looms out of the mist, and I suggest, "Maybe we'd better get off." She brakes, swings the wheel, and the car hydroplanes, bouncing violently against a curb and shuddering to a stop in the grass triangle between the on and off ramps. "Jesus!" says Dad sharply, in a tone that implies, "This is what happens when women are in charge."

The rain eases. I collect my wits and offer to drive the rest of the way. Dad states, "I'm driving if your mother's not!" She gets us back into the traffic stream, steering on to Bedford. While I sit slumped and brooding, she calls from the front, "If we were cats, we would have just used eight of our nine lives."

*M*other and Dad often play *Boggle.* You shake up a box of letters, turn the hourglass over, and try to find as many words as you can before the sands run through. Longer words get you more points. I always get nervous when asked to join in, because they're both experts. They used to have a rule that only words with four letters or more could count, but now three-letter words count as well. It's good they're doing this. Studies indicate that exercising the brain slows dementia.

Tonight, Dad wins fair and square. Before heading upstairs, he and Mother clear the game away, carefully settling the letters in their beds. My head droops like a dictionary on too thin a stalk. Muffled voices call me back to a time when I lay tucked in, listening to them as they talked downstairs, soothed as a child in the womb or an opera lover who'd rather not know what the words mean. Sometimes, I was allowed to start the night in their bed. I seemed to sleep more deeply then, and waking took longer, as though I were coming back through both of them.

Minnows of sand have passed through the hourglass. I am the one to check locks, switch off lamps, and feel my way along creaking floorboards, guided by a small bulb shining in the bathroom, a night light in the shape of a lighthouse.

Some years ago, Mother and Dad made a plan to have their ashes scattered over water. In theory, I'm not opposed to the idea, but I realize I'd rather have their ashes buried in a quiet spot and marked with a stone. Flowers thrown into the current would disappear so quickly. I've started gazing longingly at traditional cemeteries.

A genealogy Dad prepared in 1985 relates how his first ancestor in the New World was buried at sea unintentionally:

> Peter G***, Mariner, with his wife, several sons and perhaps a few daughters, came from Wales between 1620 and 1627. Peter was an admitted inhabitant of Charlestown, Massachusetts Bay, in 1637, along with seventeen others including John Harvard. He owned vessels and 'coasted' between Massachusetts Bay and Virginia and the Dutch Plantations. He died in the South while on a voyage. Before his death he requested that his body be brought north for burial. During the voyage when a severe storm arose, his coffin was swept overboard.

My reaction, completely irrational, I know—at least he was tucked into his coffin.

*M*other's Day Weekend. My husband, David, and I take Dad on an excursion to the herring run in Brewster, leaving Mother with some time alone. All these fish churning below each set of falls, so intent on returning to their birthplace—why can't they mate in random locations like the rest of us?

Dad's had enough. A few gulls saunter beside the water. "Look, he's made a catch!" I announce, as one gull lunges like a flapping dishrag. Dad smiles and nods from thirty feet back. We've barely arrived, and he can't wait to leave. Trying to corral his impatience, I stroll with him along the path. He expresses an interest in the stone mill, but the chilly rooms condense his eagerness into boredom. We're both ready to get back to the car. I'm tired of purposeful mating, and I don't want to see corn ground down.

*M*other speaks of overpopulation, how upset she is that the earth must carry more and more people. It's gotten so that she doesn't have much hope for the planet or the human race. She's not in the mood to hear that she and Dad give me faith in humanity, so I comment on the beauty of her bulbs and lilacs, and on how well the young maple is doing.

The world transforms itself through human eyes, and also through what animals see, birds, caterpillars, and crickets, and what plants sense, trillium and honey-suckle, each a witness to its portion. When we die, memories of ponds, fields, the visible tree we thought of as the whole tree, all go with us, impressions countless as leaves. The more abundant its inhabitants, the more rapidly earth escapes its chrysalis, renewing itself in the way water changes to vapor—we rain upon the earth, and, through us, earth becomes spirit.

Solar Eclipse

May 10, 1994

I'm at work in the high school language lab, when the eclipse begins. We troop outside, laughing and talking, glad for any excuse to be free, aware of the danger if we risk a direct look.

Seized by a chill, trees shiver in the departing light, newly opened leaves curled into luminous fists, and the teenagers, too, are radiant, like young foliage, showing one another how to cast shadow eclipses through an upraised fist. The sun becomes a wedding band placed against black cloth, repeating itself in myriad shadows on pavement and spring grass. Facing away, I hold out a fist and send my own eclipse to quiver among the others, imagining darkness moving steadily across my father's mind, wondering how much will be obscured, how much light will be left.

*M*y youngest sister, Andrea, and I drive south to meet Mother and Dad in Bedford for the third appointment at the Veterans Hospital. Gail, our middle sister, lives in western Pennsylvania. "This has gone on long enough!" Dad says to the doctor. He wants his driving privileges restored pronto and gives an eloquent plea in his own defense, demonstrating his acuity by reciting memories of Generals Pershing and Eisenhower. The doctor says it is not within his power to restore Dad's driving, adding gently that Dad can be the navigator, but not the driver. Distressed, Dad stands up, accuses the doctor of not listening to reason, and laments, "You have made me a very disappointed man."

I take his arm. "Come on, Dad, let's get out of here." We rush outdoors into the sun. Dad keeps repeating, "He gave me no reason. He has nothing to back him up." I tell him the family has become concerned about his memory and doesn't want anything to happen to him. He demands examples. "Well, when I visited last month, you forgot that you're the one who always makes the hot fudge sauce," I offer feebly. "And, the other day, you forgot how to fill the bird feeder." His bitter laugh demolishes my case.

We go back inside. The meeting is still in progress, but Dad is too upset to be present. Andrea offers to take him for another walk. He's inconsolable. How do you reason with someone who has problems with reasoning? Dad's search for lost privileges turns up nothing but disappointment, a common weed thriving everywhere he goes.

*T*wice, Dad has sent me a typed page titled "language lapses," a compilation of courtroom bloopers he copied out of a book by Richard Lederer. Two examples:

> Q. *Now, Mrs. Johnson, how was your first marriage terminated?*
> A. *By death.*
> Q. *And by whose death was it terminated?*

✻   ✻   ✻

> Q. *Did you ever stay all night with this man in New York?*
> A. *I refuse to answer that question.*
> Q. *Did you ever stay all night with this man in Chicago?*
> A. *I refuse to answer that question.*
> Q. *Did you ever stay all night with this man in Miami?*
> A. *No.*

Dad's always loved this kind of thing. Unaware of his own lapses, he doesn't see the irony. What's so great about irony, anyway? You reel the joke in, admire it for a moment, and throw it back. Irony is the barb that tears its way out.

⌢⌣

We grill a steak on the hibachi, which balances on an elaborate platform of planks and sawhorses rigged up by Dad. Usually, of course, we wait for the coals to cool down overnight before disposing of them. After dinner, I wander into the backyard and notice that the hibachi has been put away.

I run to find Dad and ask, "Where's the hibachi?"

He says, "Everything's fine. I emptied it behind the garage."

He's dumped burning coals next to the foundation, just below the first row of shingles. One look at my face, and he mutters, "I suppose you want me to dig it in a little more."

"I'll do it." I get the hose, water the area thoroughly, and rake the steaming coals back and forth into the sandy dirt. Every time one coal is buried, another surfaces.

> Now is the desolation of summer, when we try to take advantage of the good things life brings,
>> when sweltering bedrooms inject us with one dream after another,
>> when fire threatens to consume the firefighter,
>> when my mother swims away from my father, and he shouts in
>>> fear.
> Now is the desolation of summer, when night fills the air with fragrances as fleeting as a life looked back on.

*D*ad has been blessed with a beautiful baritone voice. In one of my most cherished childhood memories, he's bathed in a spotlight, singing "Carolina in the Morning" in the Methodist Church variety show. He also played First Lord of the Admiralty in Gilbert & Sullivan's *H.M.S. Pinafore* and can still deliver his lines lickety-split: *I polished up that handle so carefullee/That now I am the ruler of the Queen's Navee!*

This evening, we're rocking on the porch, crooning "It Had To Be You," one of Dad's favorites. I used to count on him for the words, but now he follows a half step behind, listening and plugging in those mouthed syllables choristers fall back on when they haven't learned a piece by heart. We come to a section neither of us knows, so we hum. A word jumps in like a cricket, and we hum again on slightly different notes, in the manner of all creatures trilling at sunset.

*I*n New Hampshire, my despair feeds on silence, increasing its strength when evening comes. In the woods after supper, I turn to look back upon the darkening path, half hoping to be followed by a deer, but nothing of the kind happens. When I'm this depressed, even the bats seem friendly, darker slices of the night.

All this talk of despair—like a bone found in soup, it's only worth remarking on once.

I imagine you, Dad, ferried into the underworld of myth. People there appreciate your optimism. The air is musty, the fires small, as though the dead were camping.

When I disembark, I search for you in the great tunnels, studying insubstantial faces. My ears strain for your voice, the professional voice you use away from your family. Occasionally through the years you've used that voice on me, when I've called you at the office or dropped in unexpectedly. Hurrying along, my head is filled with the joy of hearing you, first your professional voice, and then the fond voice that will mean you know me.

*M*other and Dad are up with the light. As in most marriages, one walks slightly ahead, and with their two sets of eyes they enter the outside world, drive to the mall, and find racks of clothing on sale. Dad admires a pair of lightweight outdoor shoes. Mother puts them back, saying that he can have them when it's warmer. She buys me a bathrobe the color of moss. Vigilant, a couple patrols its territory.

In the afternoon, Dad comes downstairs and says, "Katherine, there are no clothes in my closet." Mother goes up to the bedroom, and, sure enough, only two or three things dangle on hangers. She searches high and low and finally finds his clothes in the eaves. In an unremembered moment, he had opened the Alice in Wonderland door and draped them in there. What was going through his head? He loves his clothes so much, he returns to them many times each day. Perhaps he thought they were in danger, and, like a mother cat, moved them to a safer spot.

*B*ig announcement on the news. Research suggests that special eye drops might be able to show who has Alzheimer's disease and who does not. The pupils of those with the disease would dilate abnormally, as though keen to open onto chaos.

This news makes me relieved. In a few years, I'll be able to find out once and for all if the absurd errors I make can be traced to Alzheimer's. Today, I said *Cornell University* when I meant *Brown.*

I'll join the Hemlock Society, obtain the necessary pills. At odd moments, I find myself wording my good-bye letters to my sons, two different letters with different emphases. I'll say nothing of an admonitory nature. Like a bilingual speaker, I'll say *I love you* to each in his own language.

*M*y mother ties an apron on Dad whenever we eat in the dining room. He polishes off a lot of food these days, though his ceaseless activity burns the flesh from his bones. Rushing through his meal, he scatters particles this way and that, until the floor resembles the ground under a bird feeder. On one of my past visits, he leaned over during dinner, picked some crumbs off the carpet, and put them in the pickle dish. Recently, however, he seems less aware of the spills.

"Your mother has me wear this," he says sheepishly, gesturing at his apron.

After dinner, he switches on the organ. I stand behind him and start to sing along, *Are ye able, said my Master, to be crucified with me? And the sturdy dreamer answered, To the death I follow Thee!* He hasn't lost his knack for playing by ear. We move quickly through portions of a few more hymns and end with "The Star-Spangled Banner." Dad laughs and says, "Nancy, we should go on the circuit! We could make a lot of money." Before I can agree, he vanishes like an amputated limb on no particular errand, leaving a legacy of phantom pain.

*L*ast evening, I attended an open house and reception for the new Alzheimer's wing at a local nursing home. The open house didn't actually occur in the new wing; we gathered in conference rooms situated near the front door of the regular nursing home. A video and two speakers were scheduled, and quite a few people showed up. In a room smelling slightly of urine, I saw the eight-minute video, which culminated in a shot of several patients seated around a table batting a Nerf ball back and forth with feather dusters. Tours were given upon request. A man in a business suit ushered me into the presence of a pleasant woman who turned out to be the head nurse of the Alzheimer's wing. Immediately, she guided me into the hallway. "I didn't mean that I need a private tour. I can easily wait for the group," I hastily proposed. "Oh, no," she said. "We don't want to distress the patients with lots of new faces at once." I followed her through the home's disturbing landscape to a pair of doors that could be opened only by pressing a combination of numbers on the wall. Every atom in my being was on alert.

On the other side of the rainbow, we found ourselves surrounded by people who must have Alzheimer's. One jolly little woman came up and took my hand. "Aren't you the most beautiful thing I've ever seen!" she cried. Accustomed to my father's pride in me, these words weren't overly startling. Most patients had eaten, though a few were still seated with a whiff of permanence at tables draped with powder blue tablecloths. A young, bearded man holding a keyboard instrument was conferring with several patients and staff. The nurse explained that late afternoon and early evening are the most difficult times of day for those with Alzheimer's. In order to help reduce agitation, this musician comes in after supper and plays for forty-five minutes. Beginning with peppy numbers, he gradually slows the pace until a calm mood prevails.

All of the thirty-odd bedrooms were doubles, and at each door hung laminated photos, along with a list of assorted interests, hobbies, etc. "We like to use a photograph about twenty years old, if we can get it," the nurse commented. "The patients don't recognize themselves as they are now, and it helps the staff keep a sense of the person's individual worth." Hoarse shouts erupted nearby, and I was whisked away.

All told, I must have been in the Alzheimer's wing little more than five minutes. Chagrined, I realized I'd failed to go down the checklist detailing policies and privileges, for the sake of comparison, in case I end up helping Mother evaluate nursing homes on Cape Cod. One thing I'd learned—Alzheimer's patients can't tolerate announcements on a PA system. The sound coming from nowhere disorients them too much. On the whole, I received an impression of tranquillity, but perhaps that was because I distanced myself with kindness. I smiled very warmly, not once imagining that any of those people might be my relative. It strikes me how remote my father seemed during my investigations, and how difficult it is to think deeply about someone, when you're thinking about what's right.

﹏

November is National Alzheimer's Disease Month, prophetically established by Ronald Reagan himself in 1983. In a letter to "My Fellow Americans" dated November 5, 1994, he announces that he is *one of the millions of Americans who will be afflicted with Alzheimer's Disease.* I imagine our former president bent over a desk, painstakingly committing his generic optimism to paper. *At the moment I feel just fine.* That reminds me so much of Dad.

I call Mother. "This might be a good time to tell Dad he has Alzheimer's. You could say something like, 'The Alzheimer's disease that President Reagan has ... well, the doctors think that you have it, too.'"

She's against such a course, saying that Dad knows all about Reagan and hasn't made any connection to himself. I remind her that Reagan didn't necessarily figure out on his own that he has Alzheimer's—there were five specialists to tell him. It bothers me that no effort is being made to chip away at the fortress of Dad's denial. I've read that some people are relieved to receive an explanation for the loss of their abilities. Dad should be given a chance to rise to the occasion. Not knowing makes him more a victim.

Mother insists that all Alzheimer's people are victims. "Your father couldn't handle knowing," she finishes. "Don't you dare tell him."

"I won't," I promise. "You're the one who has to cope with him."

"That's right," she says.

On the six o'clock news, Nancy Reagan leads her husband by the hand past reporters. He sends a hesitant smile into the living rooms of America, but his glance falters. His eyes can't join in the message.

⌒⇀

We're walking along the winter beach,
my father and I, and I say, "Dad,
I think you should know you have Alzheimer's disease."
The tide is high, the sand frozen in prehistoric formations.
I can't take my words back—they jostle with bird cries on the way
into my father's ears. He turns, pins me with his blue eyes, and says,
"I know, Nancy, I've known for some time, but I didn't want to upset
your mother." Or he says, "Thank you for telling me,
Nancy, I suspected something was wrong." Or
he starts to cry.
Or he doesn't understand
and looks at me inquiringly.
Above us, gulls and terns balance
as though the wind were a huge tree.

*M*y parents' property is bordered by fencing and hedges. In spring, Dad is on his hands and knees, tearing out crabgrass. In autumn, he picks up every fallen leaf. Mother has banished the sharp garden tools. The ax went into his shin, and the clippers nearly sliced off the tip of his forefinger.

Indoors, he empties all the wastebaskets into a barrel in the basement, which gets emptied into another barrel in the garage. He calls it "straightening up." Mother's favorite jujube candy ends in the trash covered with coffee grounds. When challenged, he explains it's not a kind he likes. In the middle of a meal, he'll leave the table and start scraping plates at the sink, putting Mother's new washcloth with the garbage. I drape my arm around his shoulders and cajole, "Come on, Dad, we're still eating."

During the day, he judges light. On a gloomy afternoon, he'll decide that there's more light inside than out and pull down the shades halfway. Even on a decent day, Mother might have to go around letting up the shades three or four times.

Raking, weeding, emptying the wastebaskets—there are still many things Dad can do. He can stand at the window and anticipate night. He can close the eyes of the house, so that the house is forced to look inward, at him.

*M*other researches day care programs and places Dad in one that has activities for a wide range of abilities, with plenty of light streaming through the windows. He goes twice a week, Tuesday and Friday.

"I really don't know why I have to do this," he grumbles. He has to be there from nine o'clock to three o'clock, which exhausts him.

"You're doing it as a favor to me," Mother answers.

After only two weeks, he refuses to continue. Six hours is too long. It's a shame they won't accept half-days. "Oh, well," Mother says, scooping a handful of resignation from her inner lake.

Lately, for some strange reason, I've been wondering which of his three daughters he will forget first. I wish I could tell him it's okay if he forgets me first. As the oldest, I think I'd be able to handle it better. So I just want to say, Dad, if it's a help, forget me first.

I don't understand how Dad can fail to realize that something is wrong with him. Last week, even though Mother came down with a twenty-four-hour bug, she had to get up to feed him his three meals. Before, he always took care of her when she was sick. Statistics claim that ninety percent of Alzheimer's victims grieve their decline. Perhaps Dad's restlessness is a manifestation of that grief.

It would seem that the lessons of Alzheimer's are meant not for the victims, but for others. We spectators are the ones who must adjust our understanding of identity, when the self falls away. As Dad's essence intensifies, the words *identity* and *self* come to mean much more than I imagined. My father has become a flower that blooms in the darkest hour of the night. We would know nothing of this blossoming, were it not for the petals lying scattered at his feet.

*M*other calls with shocking news. During Dad's annual physical, his doctor discovered signs of an abdominal aortic aneurysm. Further tests confirmed it, and they have an appointment with a vascular surgeon next week. My fear has become a treasure I hoard and examine. Alzheimer's patients do very poorly with an interruption of routine. A hospital stay, strange nurses, an unfamiliar bed, anesthesia, all will hasten his dementia. Normally, before an operation we wish the patient luck. In the case of those with Alzheimer's disease, the wind wheels our wishes away and scatters them like milkweed rubbed between its fingers.

On the nature trail, Dad tells me how the doctor pressed down on his stomach to show him the pulsing blood vessel. He hastens to add there's an explanation for it—an Alka-Seltzer made his stomach puffy. He's sure that when he goes in for further tests next week, all symptoms will be gone.

I say to him, "Oh, well, whatever will be, will be."

We look at each other, laugh, and launch into "Que Sera, Sera." I used to think that the way to understand experience is to go deeper into it. Alzheimer's disease has taught me that sometimes you need to go toward the shallows. It's as if Dad has lost his bearings in waist-deep water, and the only way to help is to wade out, take his hand, and walk with him to shore.

*A*t the end of the weekend, I feel more than ever that this might be my last visit with Dad. When I try to say good-bye to him, I feel as though I'm floating in good-byes. Perhaps it's not possible to make a lasting gesture at the speed with which we move away from one another. Afraid I might never see him again, I torture myself with fears that my side of the good-bye is not worthy. In fact, our good-bye seems to exist separately, seizing us hastily before slipping away to join others of its kind. Dad doesn't understand how serious the aneurysm is, or that this good-bye is different—I don't know whether that makes it easier for me, or harder.

When our bodies are erased, I hope we can choose to put on our familiar faces, to help us find one another. Perhaps, for the first meeting, our spirits will wear masks adjusted loosely, like costumed children who pull at their disguises, in order to breathe.

*D*ad's operation has been postponed. After evaluating his heart, the doctors have decided the risk is too great. They don't do this kind of procedure if there's been any kind of heart attack within six months, and tests show that, unbeknownst to us, he's had one.

I go down for a quiet visit, paralyzed almost immediately by the languor that overpowers me when my parents are in control. Everything is geared to Dad, to keeping track of what he's doing, or looking for things he's misplaced, the TV guide, his glasses, the large serving spoon, the discount coupons. While Mother and I are rocking on the porch in a rare moment by ourselves, I murmur, "I wonder where Dad is."

"He's down writing in his journal."

"I didn't know he kept a journal."

"Oh, he's been doing it for a few months. I'm sure he wouldn't mind if you asked to see it."

Dad immediately fetches a small notebook and shows me some entries:

> *Had my monthly physical check up. "As usual you're in excellent shape for a man your age."*
>
> *For the 1st time I saw a star in the sky!*
>
> *Once again Kay & I walked our favorite nature trail behind the P.O. It was so quiet & lovely.*
>
> *Nancy and I had a nice walk on our favorite bridge. Trouble? It was so foggy!*

44

Loring & Lindy came over to enjoy a meal. I never met a husband and wife I loved so much. Also both Loring & Lindy have a good sense of humor!

I'm reminded of his father's diaries stored in the basement, decades of volumes containing little but the skeletons of his days. A Methodist minister and father of eight children must have had drama in his life, but his spare notations give little away. As a child, I started a few diaries, similar in their brevity, that petered out. On special trips, I'm apt to sit in the evening and jot down the day's activities as a way of savoring and preserving them. Come to think of it, that's probably what my grandfather was doing. On the occasion of a birth or death, he didn't need to go into detail or describe his feelings. With restraint, he recorded the event in his spidery hand on the day allotted, and the words pointed off the page to a realm of associations, as hymns point to heaven.

*D*ad's doctor informs Mother that the postponement has elapsed—the operation on the aneurysm can be rescheduled. She tells him they will not be going ahead with it. She feels that the quality of life he enjoys now is worth preserving as long as possible. Every day, he conveys pride in his offspring, as he calls us, and gratitude for the beauty of his surroundings.

I want to thank you, Alzheimer's disease, while you are still here to be thanked. I don't know exactly how to put it. With a double-edged sword, you've shielded Dad from harsh reality. I guess I could thank you for allowing him to sing "The Star-Spangled Banner," as you accompany him into the valley.

Dad wanders into the living room where we're watching TV, puts his hand on his heart, and starts singing to Mother, *I love you truly, truly, dear.*

He has a smile on his face. We are to understand that this is musical comedy. In our home, we don't need Shakespeare and opera to communicate the profound truths.

As David and I are saying our good-byes, I put my hand on my heart, look Dad in the eye, and sing theatrically, *I love you truly, truly, dear.*

"Oh, Nancy," he says in a broken voice, knowing I mean it.

*U*pon first hearing the term, I say, "What bed?" My friend, a psychiatric nurse, repeats, "Net bed." She explains that the ward she works on has two net beds, for occasions when Alzheimer's patients or others need to be restrained for their own safety. She goes on to describe the net, sort of like mosquito netting with big holes. I know this is something I'll have to see for myself. I go to the ward at night. The net bed is occupied by an emaciated man suffering from the DTs. The nurse addresses him, saying, "I'm showing my friend here your bed."

It's hard to tell if his muttering is intended for us. In an attempt to make him feel included, I say brightly, like a talented shopper, "I'm thinking of getting one of these beds for my father." A kind of recreational court with zippered flaps, it reminds me of tennis games with Dad. I try to picture how it would feel to be confined there, a bird in an aviary. Better than being in a strait jacket or strapped to a chair. I almost wish I had one.

I daydream of my father, who resembles Joseph Cotton, with the kind of good looks that can mean trouble. Submerged in the water at Ocean Park, Maine, he suddenly rises, sending me flying off his shoulders into a dive I still haven't completed, my hands pressed together as he has taught me. How lucky I am to have a father who loves to play—blue eyes, black hair, salt water splashing down his face—and how blind my child's eyes are to his beauty, yet somehow it is noted and preserved. Years later, I give what beauty I possess to my children, as they will to theirs, each generation unaware of the gift's value. In that way, when time pulls in its nets, beauty slips safely through.

October leaves are falling, and Dad rakes one part of the front lawn over and over. Two years ago this month, our old dog Max died of cancer. The grayer his muzzle, the more I treasured him. He was put to sleep in his own bed, head erect, radiating dignity as the needle entered his leg. When his neck relaxed, David caught his head.

The day before, I'd been seized with grave-digging fever. I chose a protected spot on the edge of the back lawn, visible from the kitchen window. Following the vet's instructions, I dug down three feet, measuring with my yardstick, clipping roots, carving perfect corners in the clay. Next morning, I lined the bottom with pine needles. The rain held off. After the vet had driven away, we wrapped Max in a white sheet, carried him to his grave, and lowered him while he was still warm. We were careful with his tail. We put in his water dish, his collar and his toys, shoveled in a thick blanket of dirt, and laid a piece of slate on top. Later, when it started to rain, I rushed out with a tarp.

This was a dog I'd sometimes treated roughly, impatiently, a terrier mix of unknown lineage I'd walked with, caressed, and complained about for nearly fifteen years. We gave one another an understandable life. I was proud of his body, his feet and penis rather big for a thirty-five-pound dog, his bedroom eyes, his chin whiskers that hid pills, his tail that wagged in circles instead of back and forth. He could be a black and white blur, or as slow as a local train. I held his face in my hands, kissed his nose, and said good-bye. For so long, I looked into the future to study his death. Now, still unprepared, I must look into the past.

The paths Max wore away in his years of guarding us are grown over, though I keep thinking I see him limping toward me. The lawn raked bare will grow again. The leaves will accumulate, and no one will try to remove every single one. The days will drift down, the day my father dies among them, a fragile veil similar to the others, as if all from the same tree.

On my way to the Cape before Christmas, the snow-tipped hills of New Hampshire gleam like whitecaps. I drive with dread, not knowing what tensions await me. The weekend before, Mother found Dad in the kitchen on his hands and knees, "cleaning" the new no-wax vinyl floor with coarse sandpaper.

Penguins on TV struggle to shore. I tell Dad about the baby penguin I bought at the Biodôme in Montreal, confessing that, when I sleep alone, I take the penguin to bed. Later, I find propped on my pillow the teddy bear Mother gave him. Devastated, I hug it fiercely, while my mind ranges far from my arms: *Now my future grief will be unmanageable. It would be easier if he were more incapable.* In the land bordering death, selfish thoughts are natural vegetation growing in such profusion, and with such disarming appeal, that one is to be forgiven for gathering them in bouquets.

Dad and I go to church together, while Mother stays behind to cook for relatives who are coming over. Presenting himself in clothes selected days in advance, he looks truly handsome, except for one minor flaw: instead of a handkerchief, he's folded a tie so that the end sticks out of his jacket pocket in a triangle. Mother chuckles and sends him up for a handkerchief, but he comes back with a different tie. Eventually, a handkerchief is found. The church service features a "sermon-in-song," through which he sits quietly, giving rein to his exuberance only during the three hymns, boisterous selections celebrating the coming of Christ. *HARK! THE HERALD ANGELS SING,* he shouts. *JOY TO THE WORLD! THE LORD IS COME.* Worshippers four aisles ahead turn around. *GOD REST YOU MERRY, GENTLEMEN, LET NOTHING YOU DISMAY!* Unable to hear my own voice, I struggle to stay on key. These hymns don't seem to be pitched for ordinary mortals. I haven't got a key that I know of, but, if I did, it wouldn't be this one. At the end of the service, we head for the coat rack. Though all men's raincoats look the same to me, the one Dad puts on seems to be for a much shorter man. We paw through until we find one he says is his for sure, because it has a clothespin in the pocket. Mother later explains that they usually fasten clothespins on their collars, for easy identification.

Turning Dad over to Mother, I relax a little, not to true relaxation, but to some state above it, like a gull far from land, waiting for the sea to calm.

I don't know if Dad has thoughts about death. He thinks about bowling, why not death? I don't ask for a long discussion, just some shared sense of this unfathomable event, but the idea of mentioning it makes me uneasy. With two older siblings alive past ninety, he may not feel pressured.

In a sense, Dad has walked through his life in much the same way that he walks the nature trail, with appreciation, undisturbed by imponderables. I tag along like a slow pupil who writes everything down, though the lesson is not in words. And I'm not the only one with an interest—skirting trees, eavesdropping from behind shrubbery, a henchwoman sent by the Lord of Darkness cranes to catch the gist, were Dad to talk about death. I can imagine Dad ushering her to the inside of the sidewalk, saying, as he has said to me, "According to the book, a man should walk to his partner's left, to protect her."

Easter weekend. Dad comes up behind me in the kitchen and intones,

> *When I consider how my light is spent,*
> *E're half my days, in this dark world and wide,*
> *And that one Talent which is death to hide,*
> *Lodg'd with me useless, though my soul more bent*
> *To serve therewith my Maker . . .*

"I learned that years ago in school," he laughs. Sensing my confusion, he fetches an old book of Milton's poetry and shows me the sonnet, which ends, *They also serve who only stand and waite.* At the moment, I stand and wash dishes.

Dad wins both games of horseshoes Saturday morning. Gallant as ever, he says, "You know, it's not often I get to play with such a beautiful ..."

I grin. "Oh, sure."

BuSpar, the anti-anxiety drug he's been taking three times a day, hasn't reduced his agitation. With the doctor's permission, Mother doubles the dose to two with every meal. "I've gone this long without these pills," Dad complains. "I don't know why I have to start now."

Catering to his fondness for lifesavers, I present him with an Easter gift, a "Sweet Storybook" containing eight rolls of different flavors, from Topical Fruit and Butter Rum to Wild Cherry. Before long, he's unwrapped all the rolls, eaten an assortment, and distributed the rest with his bowling gear and in covered dishes around the house. Canada Mints, caramels, and licorice used to be his favorite candies, but lifesavers have come from behind like a long shot. He buys a roll every time he goes with me to get the paper. I was told as a child that lifesavers got their name because you can breathe through the hole, if one gets stuck in your throat.

Monday morning, we awake to an April snowstorm. Knowing I have to get back to New Hampshire, Dad is determined to shovel the driveway. Worried about his aneurysm, I want to do it myself, but I might as well try to stop a runaway locomotive. While I'm still in my robe, he slings on his winter gear and heads for the door. "Take small amounts at a time," Mother calls after him. "Don't tell me how to do my job," he retorts, slamming his way out.

If you grasp the table's reality then you see that in the table itself are present all those things which we normally think of as the non-table world. If you took away any of those non-table elements and returned them to their sources—the nails back to the iron ore, the wood to the forest, the carpenter to his parents—the table would no longer exist.

—Thich Nhat Hanh

*I*n *The Miracle of Mindfulness*, Thich Nhat Hanh, Vietnamese Zen master, reminds us of the interdependence of all things. Carefully, he pries the table apart, showing that it is the table's nature to participate wholly in the non-table world.

My father's mind is becoming non-mind, as each skill returns to its source. Recuperating from the ceaseless flow of matter, non-elbows lean on non-tables overlooking an eternal savanna, where death is a gazelle fleeing the immeasurable force of love that calls it prey.

When I was a child, I sat with my mallet at a pegboard built into a little table and pounded colored pegs into their holes until they fell through, like sunsets. Red pegs, yellow pegs, some sliding with more difficulty than others, struggling against the resistance life offers as it encircles us.

Open photo albums lurk in every room like moths on wool. When no one's looking, I gather an armful and stuff them back in the file cabinet in the eaves. We'd hoped Dad might forget about them, if we hid them from sight. No such luck. I always assumed that the effort of taking photographs would be rewarded in the future, when we would enjoy remembering. Now, I'm not so sure. I seem to find more sadness than pleasure in looking at pictures of us when we were younger.

Who could have predicted that the architect of our family's past, the one who painstakingly assembled all these albums, would plunder them? His destruction isn't intentional—if asked what he has done with missing pictures, he doesn't know what you're talking about and is eager to help you look. They may have been thrown out, for all we know, or mailed to distant relatives. In the den, irreplaceable photos rimmed with scissors marks are taped to the walls along with scenic postcards. Mother's given up trying to save the wallpaper. "You could put a child through college on what we spend on tape," she observes. I guess it wouldn't be right to lock the albums away from the one person they mean the most to, yet it's very hard to watch the orderly past go down the drain.

Photographs are like brain cells, each one a memory that can be lost. Even unidentified photographs have such power that we may be prompted, in a secondhand shop, to buy the image of a stranger caught in a dusty frame. If some of my family's photos are ruined because my father can't leave them alone, so be it. I've come to believe that his abiding interest outweighs anyone else's claim. After he's gone, the ones that are missing won't matter, compared to the ones he showed me again and again.

*D*ad has gotten worse since I saw him last month. About two weeks ago, he didn't feel well in the afternoon. His temperature registered *102°*. Next morning, he seemed recovered, so Mother figured it was just a virus. However, we didn't realize how much harm any kind of physical problem, no matter how minor, can cause to someone with Alzheimer's. It's become more difficult to get through to him, particularly when he's engaged in an activity such as raking. If the table is set with bread, he thinks that's the whole meal and says wistfully, "I wish there was more food." On a walk at low tide, arms draped across each other's shoulders, he turns to me and asks pleasantly, "Now, are you my oldest granddaughter?"

David and I are awakened by shouts and curses coming from the backyard. At first, I don't recognize the voice. Mother's already out the door, and a moment later she comes around the garage holding the cat. It seems that Dad was practicing horseshoes, and Sheba, who follows him everywhere, insisted on standing in the way. Ordinarily, Dad would have found the cat's behavior funny, but today it provoked what the medical books call "a catastrophic reaction," that is, excessive and overly emotional.

On Sunday, rather than going to church, we drive to the nature trail. Dad calls out the states on the license plates he spots. Mother thinks he may be replaying a game he enjoyed as a child. "New Hampshire! They have a crazy saying on their plates!"

"I have that on mine," I remind him. "*Live Free or Die.* That's the way we like it up in New Hampshire."

"That's why you're still alive," he wisecracks.

Going past the church, Dad remarks that the parking lot is full of cars. Aware that he doesn't like to miss church, I say, "You can be with God on the nature trail—you don't necessarily have to be in church, right, Dad?"

"That is a very profound and true statement," he agrees. "There's more than one way to skin a cat."

Mother makes an appointment at the Veterans Hospital in Bedford after a two-year hiatus, because they no longer will fill Dad's prescriptions unless they see him. The savings are significant. We dread telling Dad. He tends to remember the very things you wish he would forget, such as the fact that the Veterans Hospital doctor took away his license. Mother breaks it to him in private the night before. He accepts his fate and doesn't become agitated until we leave the highway and approach the hospital. By the time we're seated in the waiting room, he's nervous and preoccupied. Mother asks him if he's okay. He says he's going over answers in his mind, in preparation for the test—he knows that one of the answers is "Generals Pershing and Eisenhower."

"You'd better wait to see what the questions are," Mother advises with a smile. When an orderly comes in to inform us that there will be a few more minutes' wait, Dad jumps up and zaps him with: *What kind of noise annoys an oyster? A noisy noise annoys an oyster!*

In the conference room, Dad shakes the doctor's hand and says, "Now here's a familiar face." With four professionals looking on, he launches into a tirade about his driving privileges, listing his credentials and how his work required him to drive all over New England. While he's out of the room for psychological testing, Mother brings the staff up to date, mentions the aneurysm, and concludes by describing Dad's regression since the recent virus. I jump in to tell them about his catastrophic reaction with the cat, excuse the pun. The doctor smiles broadly. Looking around at the staff, he says, "I haven't heard that one. That's good! I'm going to use that."

Dad returns from the testing with a jubilant air. "Here's a guy you like the moment you meet him!" he says of the psychologist. Relieved to have the appointment behind us, we decide to stop at the nursing home in Plymouth to visit Dad's ninety-year-old sister, Miriam, who has been in decline since breaking her hip. Dad's very excited at the prospect of seeing her. I'm unprepared for the shrunken figure that has replaced the vigorous woman I once knew. Glued to a Cary Grant movie, she acknowledges us when we enter and goes back to watching the screen. With the enunciation of a stage actress, Mother identifies us by name. Dad stands in front of the wheelchair and says, "Miriam, how do you like my pants?" Miriam looks up and says, "Oh, Gilbert," in the exasperated, fond voice of an older sister. She knows him! I say to Mother, "Maybe I should turn off the tv." "No," Mother says. "It doesn't matter." Dad pats Miriam's face and shoulders and strokes her hair, rejoicing, "She's my sister! This is my sister."

Bodies from TWA Flight 800 lost in the sea, bodies from the ValuJet crash sucked below the surface of the Everglades, never to be reclaimed, never to receive a parting kiss. Bereft families hang suspended between death and grief.

Since these tragedies, I've heard people say they don't understand why the families want the bodies back so much. "The spirit has departed," they insist. "It's just a body."

Just a body. But the body has a spirit, too, the same spirit that inhabits seashells, iridescent nests shining in the water's branches with the memory of once-held life. Much of my father's spirit has flowed into his body, to fill the hollows left by disease. I touch him often, for solace, seeming to touch spirit more than flesh.

Of course, we need the bodies. At death, the body's spirit departs slowly, having much to occupy it. We can gather the body in our arms and say, *Good-bye, I love you.* Each touch is a thought to the body's spirit. The impatient soul hurries ahead, turning to wait for the body's spirit to catch up, because the soul misses the body, though the two often have been at odds. The soul throws a comforting arm around the body's spirit, and they go forward together, the body's spirit with a dragging step, the soul like quicksilver.

We need the bodies.

*T*hree and a half years after the initial, probable diagnosis, Mother tells Dad that he has Alzheimer's disease, at the end of a difficult week during which he breaks a fitting on his hearing aid, one of his molars must be extracted, and he loses the cord to one razor and dismantles the new replacement. At the end of her rope, she goes into the bedroom and sobs. Dad leaves typed notes around the house, saying how sorry he is. When she finds them, she sits him on the bed next to her and says, "I get upset sometimes, but it's not your fault. You have Alzheimer's disease. Your brain scrambles everything up, and it's not your fault." They lie down together, and Dad weeps. Afterward, they take a walk. Mother says telling Dad has lifted a great weight off her shoulders. Dad hasn't mentioned it again.

While visiting a friend, I see a dead whale at low tide, slapped and shaken by the waves as if the sea were a mother trying to revive her child. Its skin is the color of milky tea, and I wonder in awe if this could be an albino. I'm told it only means that the whale has been dead for some time.

The whale faces away in the rain. I can see the injury that killed it, a gash down its midsection caused, probably, by a ship's propeller. The intestines, washed clean, intertwine like heavy rope, the two halves of the whale seemingly joined by the fingers of clenched hands. I want to see the eyes, but it would mean taking off my shoes and socks, and the autumn day is raw. It's pure luck I've seen this much.

I'm in Hull, on my way home from a visit to my parents. The whale is a sidewalk vendor in my heart's city. No need to cross the street to search his eyes.

Here it was something less
Than night and less than day, so that my vision
Reached only a little way ahead of us ...
—The Inferno of Dante
Canto XXXI

Winter, *1997.* Dad tells me how much more relaxed Mother is since her recent cataract surgery. As a result, everyone is more relaxed. I find myself releasing some of my nervous control. Instead of going into the village store with him to buy candy, I wait outside. If he can't figure out the money, they'll help. In the library, I let him disappear into the stacks alone to select his books. I used to accompany him, to prevent him from tossing rejects on the lower shelves. After all, I remind myself, the librarians are there to deal with this sort of thing. Dad got enthused about the large-print books Mother read while her eye was healing. She doesn't need them anymore, but he prefers them. "Your mother's surprised I finish these books so fast," he grins, holding up an Erle Stanley Gardner.

His level of confusion fluctuates wildly. From time to time, he repeats, "I can't see the forest because of the trees." Watching TV, he inquires, "Excuse me for asking, but do you have a boyfriend back where you are?" He bounds into the kitchen, where Mother is puttering around, and returns to the living room, announcing with a smile, "I'm very much in love with your mother. I had to go in and give her a kiss." Sitting back down, he muses, "My sister Miriam used to be a lot of fun. But, the last time we visited her at the nursing home, she didn't even speak to me. I asked her a question, and she didn't answer. Her mind is all jumbled up."

"That's a shame," I commiserate, not bothering to remind him that I was there for the past two visits. Miriam can't be counted on for repartee.

"It happens in the best of families," he says diplomatically. To clear the air of sad subjects, he whistles a cheerful military tune.

On the drive to the Veterans Hospital, dismal weather mirrors my mood. Rain pounds down, and my knee aches from accelerating through haze. Dad's quiet in the back seat, staring at the drenched landscape like a convict.

After a brief greeting at the round table, I take him for a walk in the corridors, while Mother talks with the assembled experts. When we rejoin the group, the doctor informs us of some new advances we should be aware of. He recommends that Dad go on 800 mg./day of Vitamin E. There's been a lot in the papers about Vitamin E's antioxidant properties. Antioxidants neutralize free oxygen radicals (byproducts of the process that converts oxygen into energy), which are implicated in the formation of plaques and tangles. He tells us about a new drug called Aricept, which increases the amount of acetylcholine in the brain. Acetylcholine is a chemical that nerve cells use in the transmission of messages, and research has shown that Alzheimer's brains don't have enough of it. After giving some brochures to Mother and encouraging her to speak to their general practitioner, the doctor addresses Dad directly: "Wouldn't you be willing to take one little pill a day?"

"What's it for?" Dad says, jolted from inattention.

"It might help your memory!" the doctor suggests with forced jocularity.

Dad lurches to his feet. "I'll have to say, *No!* There's nothing wrong with my memory!"

I stand with him. "We don't have to stay in here. Let's go walk again." We hurry down the corridor.

Dad is incensed. "I hate that guy! He's the one who pointed his finger at me and took away my driver's license. He acts like he's an emperor."

"He does have an unfortunate way about him," I agree.

"There's nothing wrong with my memory," he insists. "Everyone who gets older forgets things from time to time."

I look at him. I don't know what to say.

"I'd rather die than go back there," he tells me.

I show Mother the three puzzles I found at Kay-Bee Toy & Hobby, *100*, *60*, and *24* pieces. She thinks the one with *24* pieces would be a good place to start. Dad used to be good at *500*- and *1000*-piece puzzles. Now that he's lost interest in typing, this might keep him occupied on a rainy day. These junior puzzles are oriented to children, with scenes from Disney movies, in this case Pocahontas greeting a raccoon.

We spread the pieces on the butcher block island, and Mother calls him into the kitchen. "Look what Nancy brought."

"Oh, this looks complicated," he says.

"Let's try it," Mother encourages. "I'm not very good at this," he warns, standing with his hands in his pockets, as she puts together a few pieces. I retreat to the front hall. He does better when he's alone with her. Peeking around the corner, I see him leaning over the puzzle, a piece clutched in his hand. Mother says, "Good work!"

Later on, I take the puzzle apart, move it to the dining room, and arrange the pieces near to where they belong. Mother and I take turns doing a little with him, to keep him engaged, and undo it when he's not looking. At one point, he comes into the kitchen and announces, "I'm proud of myself!"

"What?" we ask with one voice. He motions us into the dining room. He's done the whole puzzle!

The day before I'm to leave, Mother and I are relaxing with cups of tea. Dad makes a pass through the kitchen, announcing in a loud voice, "Too bad it got broken!" Mother and I look at each other. This sounds bad. Mother tiptoes after him into the dining room.

It turns out he's referring to the puzzle I'd disassembled moments before, Pocahontas reaching to touch the raccoon's outstretched paw, like God reaching out to Adam—a spark, a welcome leaping along nerves, when the pieces are all there.

A piercing yowl sets our hair on end. Traveling through the kitchen, Dad has stepped on the cat again.

"I found something funny in a book I'm reading about Alzheimer's disease," I say to Mother.

"Oh?"

"It says that pets should be trained not to get underfoot."

Mother and I stare at each other. This is humor that vibrates at a deeper level than laughter. We stare at Sheba, now recuperating in her favorite place in front of the sink. Overweight and social, she always stretches out where the action is. You'd be wise to give her a wide berth—a gorgeously attired potentate, she's apt to swipe at your ankle for no apparent reason. Sheba has *us* trained, not the other way around.

Sheba favors Dad. This is between the two of them.

Dad marvels at the blossoms on the small-leaf rhododendrons around town, so Mother and I drive to a nursery and buy him one. What a production getting the thing in the ground, a potted shrub the size of a big head requiring peat moss, manure, wheelbarrow, watering can, shovel, trowel, just like a baby taken on a day's outing. Satisfied, we back off and regard it fondly.

Someday, this bush will remind us of a time when Dad took pleasure in beauty. If Mother carries through with her plan to scatter his ashes over water, maybe I could persuade her to save a handful to encircle this little fellow close to the ground, who came to us sporting many sunbonnets.

I attend a lecture at the nursing home on the pathology of Alzheimer's disease. We're shown slides of normal brains juxtaposed with brains shrunken like nutmeats in their shells, and images from an electron microscope of senile plaques and flame-like neurofibrillary tangles. Parts of the brain seem to vanish like dunes along a coast, beach plum, plover's nest washed away as the waters rise, turning creeks into rivers, ponds and lakes into swamp, a region's eyes gone blind.

The importance of autopsies is emphasized, both for research and for the families. Before too long, there may be preventive therapies available, making it important to know whether a family has a history of the disease. There's a good possibility that Dad's mother was a victim of Alzheimer's. I dearly hope Dad dies before he reaches the last stage, described in books as a ghastly vegetative state. The more of himself he takes with him, the better, like a child sleeping over at a best friend's house for the first time, loaded down with many things from home, though the friend has all those things, too.

Viewing the telltale plaques and tangles
in x-rays of diseased brains such as my father's,
I'm reminded of a small tree
I saw from the highway,
branches so draped
with webworm shrouds
I couldn't tell
what manner
of tree
it was.

Singing with me in the living room, Dad teases, "I'm afraid you're unfortunate enough to have inherited some of my genes. Too bad for you!"

He can't wait to show me the mountain laurel on the nature trail, thousands of shimmering pink and white blossoms joined at the stem in separate bouquets, as if he came early and tied them himself. "Look, Nancy! There's another one." He laughs with delight, as bush after bush sails into view. On the drive down, I'd stopped to see a friend and let drop that it might be a blessing if Dad died. How could I ever say that?

Perhaps hearing my comment, death comes to browse. At supper, Dad gags. Eating fast and neglecting to chew and swallow, he's managed to stuff half a ham and cheese sandwich into his throat. He stands up, his body searching for air, heaving. Mother jumps from her chair and grabs him from behind. I run for the dishpan. She does the Heimlich maneuver, forcing out matted gobs. It seems an eternity before he finds breath. "Okay, okay," he gasps, sinking to his chair. Mother and I stand over him, panting like lifeguards over a rescued swimmer. "I'm sorry," he apologizes.

In the living room, I put on a tape of Glen Miller's "Chattanooga Choo Choo." Dad starts to rock and roll. I consider getting up and dancing with him, but I stay in my chair, unwilling to take on the weight of such a happy memory. When Mother comes in, he swings into ballroom mode, holding her close but not too close, waiting for the right beat, guiding her into a fox-trot from the old days, step and over, back and left, with a little jig thrown in that she's ready for.

Sometimes, I don't know whether to laugh or to cry. At one meal, we order fish dinner take-out from Captain Frosty's, which comes with clam dumplings. Dad pokes at one, holds it up gingerly, and inquires, "What part of the body is this?"

He and I go shopping at the drugstore for Mother's birthday gift. At home, I wrap the refrigerator-magnet memo pad, while he watches. I'm afraid I'm helping him so much, he won't consider it his gift. For a hiding place, he slides open the silverware drawer and tucks it on top of the knives, forks, and spoons.

Each morning, after locating his reading glasses, pencil, and a dog-eared paperback dictionary, he settles down to do the crossword puzzle in the *Cape Cod Times*. *Great* does service for a three-letter word for *energy*, and also for a four-letter word for *seek the America's Cup*.

"What's a word of three letters for *frivolous gal of song?*" he asks.

"I don't know."

"Ah!" He jabs in an answer.

"What?"

"*Mary.*"

"But that has four letters."

"That's okay," he explains. "I made them fit."

*M*other's offered to replace two library books that Dad defaced. When he spots what he considers a spelling error or poor grammar, he runs a heavy line through it and writes the correction above. I caught him reaching for a ballpoint pen and cautioned, "That's a library book, Dad." Frustrated, he threw the pen on the floor. Once an English teacher, always an English teacher.

In a large-print western, for example, in a sentence such as, *Put down that durned gun, mistuh,* Dad will have crossed out *durned* and *mistuh* and crowded in the proper spelling, causing the text to resemble the first draft of an eighth grade homework assignment.

The librarian won't let Mother pay for the books. For Dad's eighty-fifth birthday next month, I've bought him a large-print mystery he can write in to his heart's content—*Cat Crimes II* will provide the perfect laboratory, with sentences such as, *Arly! You got to do something! Somebody's gonna get killed if you don't do something!* *Cat Crimes I* wasn't available. Somebody else got to it first.

*D*uring a phone conversation, Gail relates what occurred when Dad took her into the cemetery to show her the new grave of one of his buddies. Unable to remember the name, but sure of the general location, he searched here and there and then dredged up the professional voice that still holds weight, though shakily, like a leaky pail used for a stool.

"They must have moved it," he informed her. "They do that sometimes, you know."

"Oh, I doubt it," Gail said.

"There it is!" Dad exclaimed.

Back at home, Dad told Mother that he'd found the grave. "They'd moved it," he added.

*M*other gets out the Christmas decorations. With care, Dad arranges the manger, crowding the Angel, Shepherd, Sheep, Cow, Donkey, Wise Men, and Holy Family inside, as though everyone sought the overhang in a downpour. Mother's a whirl-wind, cutting boughs for the mantel, gathering pine needles, plugging in a candle for each window. Mostly, I get underfoot.

"You've done a wonderful job," Dad compliments me when the dust settles. I suspect, not for the first time, that he's confusing me with Mother.

"It was nothing," I quip.

"That's because I did it," Mother says under her breath.

He's in his recliner, holding the ten-year-old photograph of his three daughters sitting on a smooth boulder at the Basin in the White Mountains.

"Nancy, Gail, Andrea, Nancy, Gail, Andrea, Nancy, Gail, Andrea, Nancy, Gail, Andrea, Nancy, Gail, Andrea, Nancy, Gail, Andrea, Nancy, Gail, Andrea, Nancy, Gail, Andrea, Nancy, Gail, Andrea, Nancy, Gail, Andrea ..." he recites under his breath.

"I have a picture of you at home that I like to look at," I say, smiling.

"You do?" he says in a pleased tone and jokes, "I hope you keep it in a room you don't go in very often."

Retiring to the narrow cot in the den, he naps with the compe-tence of an effigy. I'm gripped by the tenderness that can stun us when we watch someone sleep. Under his plaid shirt, his chest lifts as imperceptibly as a calm sea. Who can say where we are swept on that inner journey, or what reassurances we are given? Last night, I went to sleep afraid of death, yet woke this morning unafraid. What if death is merely an usher who escorts us from our body's chapel into a cathedral? Perhaps memory is a hymn known to the choir, sung for those who want to remember. Death is not the equal of light. To add its few brush strokes, death calls for a torch.

"I'll be frank with you," Dad says to Mother, gesturing toward his Jell-O salad on a bed of lettuce. "I don't know how to eat this."

"You can start by taking the pieces of lettuce one by one with your fingers," she suggests.

Dad makes it through his salad and glances at the TV. The words *weak trough* are superimposed over a map of the coast. "*W E A K,*" Dad spells aloud, taking one letter at a time, like pieces of lettuce. "What's that?"

On an excursion in the car, he praises my driving: "You're as good a driver as your mother! Gosh, you don't know how much I miss driving. *Live Free or Die*—I guess that means I'm going to die." We point out sights to one another and stop to admire the view over the ocean. He gets nostalgic about Vermont, where I was born. "You're my Montpelier daughter," he says with certainty. After a companionable silence, he faces me and says, "I love you." "I love you, too," I say, squeezing his knee. My voice sounds forced to me, false somehow, not as pure as his. He's caught me by surprise, his words the deepest water from the well, upon which all other waters rest.

I can't imagine life without Dad. I can't imagine walking the nature trail without him, driving around town, or watching the tide from the wooden bridge. All the ways I will miss him blur together like a view seen through tears, forcing me to go slowly, one at a time. Loss mesmerizes the survivors, seeping through hills of muscle, fences of bone, settling in the marrow like flecks of gold in a stream, so that, ever afterward, sorrow must be present if the landscape is to please us.

*E*aster. Dad and Mother were on their feet singing a hymn in their usual pew, fourth from the rear, when Dad collapsed. Face rigid, eyes fixed open, he slumped against Mother, legs twitching as if impatient to get away. While the service continued, several folks came to their aid. By the time a wheelchair was brought, he'd recovered enough to get feisty. The emergency team arrived from the fire station across the street, strapped him into their own portable wheelchair, and whisked him down the church stairs, onto a stretcher, and into the ambulance. Mother followed in her car.

In the emergency room, the tests came back showing no problems. It was just a matter of getting the doctor to sign off. Easier said than done. After two hours, the doctor still hadn't been located. Trapped by an IV, Dad was frantic to get home. A nice nurse brought them sandwiches and chased down the doctor, who signed off on Dad without seeing him. Mother noticed that he wrote *fainting fit* for the diagnosis. "If that was a fainting fit, I'll eat my hat," Mother told the nurse. We think it was a TIA (transient ischemic attack), a kind of mini-stroke that leaves no trace. He's suffered several of varying strengths over the years, none this public.

On the phone Mother sounds drained. The second hour spent waiting for the doctor was the worst part of the whole thing for her. She says she was too tired last night to eat supper, so she made Dad some soup, and a cup of tea for herself. Dad's in a state of outrage. He keeps saying, "If you'd only asked me, Katherine, I could have told you there was nothing wrong with me."

"He brings it up constantly. Finally, I hollered at him."

"Of course you did," I say.

"Too bad it didn't happen during the 'Hallelujah Chorus,'" she adds. "We just missed it."

Nothing like Handel to drown out the opposition.

*T*hinking to get some tips for Mother, I attend a stress workshop supposedly geared to Alzheimer caregivers, but I guess I'm too stressed to put up with the laid-back guru leading it. We're each asked what we hope to get out of the class, and one woman, a nurse, says she finds it stressful when a particular patient on her ward asks the same question repeatedly. "Why do you find that stressful?" our leader prompts.

"Well, I'm trying to get meds for twenty-six people, and she keeps interrupting me." Is our leader dense, or am I overreacting?

How would we feel, he wants to know, if we were standing in a long movie line and a man barged in front of us and even stepped on our toe? We throw out words to describe how we would feel—*angry, resentful*—and then we're offered a different version. What if we notice that he is wearing dark glasses and carrying a white cane. How does that make us feel? *Guilty,* we cry. We understand that our stress comes from an incorrect perception. If we'd known the man were blind, we gladly would have offered him a place in line. I know where this is headed. We can lower our stress by reminding ourselves that we are dealing with behavior caused by a disease. I also know that this simple solution won't benefit Mother. She's perfectly aware that Dad can't help himself. Try living with a roommate called Alzheimer for years without building up stress. Where do you put it? I'll tell you where you don't put it. You don't entrust it to a person who drops off a rude blind man at the movies and drives away.

On the wall of Dad's basement study is a typed copy of a poem he wrote in the early 1950s:

LINES IN PRAISE OF LITTLE GIRLS

My heart inclines to little girls;
I like their pigtails, bangs and curls,
Their stunts and riddles and surprises
Sprung in different daily guises,
Their pride in prowess when they've won.
I just think little girls are fun.

I like their sweet, wide, toothy grins,
Their alibis for little sins,
Their rash defiance and their glee,
Their questions which embarrass me.
I like their easy, loping gait.
I just think little girls are great!

He doesn't want his typewriter in the house anymore. "Let's sell it," he suggests. "I haven't used it for five or ten years."

"No one will want it," Mother says. "Everyone uses computers now."

I go down to the basement and locate the typewriter, a pitiful relic held together with masking tape, from the days when Mother tried to discourage him from messing with the ribbon. It's been moved from his study to the workbench area. I don't like the idea of either of them lifting it.

"I'll take it with me," I announce. Mother finds the case, and I lug it into the car. On the drive north, the typewriter rocks back and forth like a small boat with many ribs, each letter encrusted

84

with barnacles of dust and carbon, the last voyage of a faithful companion who waited patiently for Dad in the basement and never questioned where they would go.

*S*canning Father's Day cards facing me like rows of cadets, I search for something Dad would like. Passing over the golfer, the fisherman, the handyman, the backyard chef as too intellectual, I select a forest scene, featuring eyes peering from dense vegetation. *HAPPY FATHER'S DAY, DAD*, it says on the front, and, on the inside, superimposed over a pop-out tribe of monkeys swinging off vines, *from the whole swinging bunch!*

In my parents' house, greeting cards, printed or homemade, have never been optional. Various sentiments mill around on the mantelpiece, funny, religious, romantic, a bouquet of messages devoted to one special day. The cards arrive in good time, not too early, and definitely not too late, demonstrating a certain organization that reflects well on a family. There are those who think that buying greeting cards is beneath them. I understand how they feel. I, too, have chafed against the obligation to commemorate everything with some corny card, as if we're all targets of a conspiracy cooked up by the greeting card industry. But you only have to see the delight on my father's face when he opens a card to know there's another side of the story. Some of us need a card to act as translator, in clear language, comprehensible to all but the most lost. Dad doesn't read every word, but the card itself is a word, and more than a word, for we have come to a time when words themselves are nothing, and we need something we can touch.

～✕

I call to wish Dad a happy Father's Day. Mother answers, and we chat while he wakes up from a nap. She tells me what happened when she tried to get him to wear the silver identification bracelet she got from the Alzheimer's Association, with the Association's logo on the front, and Dad's first name, the fact that he's memory impaired, and the 800 number of the central registry on the back. About an hour after she'd fastened it on him, she heard pounding in the basement and found that he'd punctured the skin on his wrist, in an effort to smash the clasp with a screwdriver and hammer. He's not one for jewelry.

He comes on the line. "Nancy?"

"Hi, Dad. Happy Father's Day!"

"I haven't seen you for so long. I love you like crazy!" Dad says.

"I love you, too!"

"I love all my Father's Day cards," he rushes on. "They make me feel great." My response is interrupted by a flood of nervous talk that creates the impression of a conversation. He winds down, and silence reigns. "Can you think of anything to say?"

"No," I admit.

"I'll hand you over to your mother, then."

Dad has started leaving the yard without telling Mother. The first time, he took off while she was getting dressed in the morning. She got in the car, drove toward the village store, and found him on the sidewalk, headed home. Another time, he suggested a walk around the block, and she said, no, it was too hot, and told him to sit on the porch. A few minutes later, she went to check and saw him rounding the end of the driveway. The most frightening time, he simply disappeared. She enlisted the help of a neighbor, who was about to set out on his bike, when Mother caught sight of Dad down the street at the corner of the cemetery.

I'm haunted by an eighty-one-year-old Vermont man with Alzheimer's disease who said to his wife after lunch, "I think I'll take a little walk."

"Okay, but no further than the end of the driveway," she reminded him.

While she read the paper, he vanished. Rescue workers, volunteers, Civil Air Patrol cadets, and search dogs scoured the hilly terrain covered with thick brush. More than a year has passed, and he hasn't been found, neither his body nor his bones.

⌒

*I*n July, Dad and I go for a walk on the trail that leads off Alms House Lane. I've come to prefer it to the nature trail behind the post office, where last spring's rain exposed numerous roots I'm afraid he'll trip over. I also prefer it to a route where we run into people. He raises his hat and feels obligated to speak— "You look younger than you did last year," or, "You look five years younger!" The passerby, perhaps leaning on a cane or bent over with arthritis, responds good-naturedly, "I doubt that."

The Alms House Lane trail is usually deserted, close to the shore, with a scenic lookout. Poison ivy has begun to encroach on the path. Dad's ahead of me, shuffling with legs slightly apart. Unable to get his attention, I watch the shiny leaves brush against his sneakers and long pants. He's very susceptible to poison ivy. Even if it doesn't touch his skin directly, he'll get the oil on his hands when he takes off his sneakers at home. Oh, well, I'll worry about that later. "Lazy boys," Dad grunts, poking his finger at a secondary trail that heads off into the bushes. It's probably a shortcut. I've never been on it, because only lazy boys would go that way.

On the last stretch, he wilts. I stick a blossom of Queen Anne's Lace in his third buttonhole, where it perches like a medal of honor. After we've washed our hands thoroughly, Dad finds Mother, points at his shirtfront, and says proudly, "I'll have to take care of this."

*D*ad intensifies his efforts to place himself and others. Every waking moment he jousts with the unknown, his opponent resplendent in full armor, Dad in his worn cardigan of a masculine design, mustard, blue, and brown, with maroon diamonds. Using indirect questions, he's developed a strategy for filling in the blanks. Like a fly fisherman, he casts in a likely direction:

> *How was the traffic from where you were coming?*

> *When you get back where you come from, what will you have to do?*

> *How do you occupy yourself nowadays?*

> *What kind of a situation awaits you on your return?*

> *Do you have any brothers and sisters?*

He no longer remembers the identities of the three attractive ladies in the photograph by his chair. "Nancy is your daughter. Andrea and Gail are her sisters. You are their father," Mother recites.

"Good for me," Dad says.

More than once, he mentions being surrounded by women. On a walk with me to buy the paper, he goes into a dialogue with himself: "Do you know Nancy? How could I not know Nancy! She's that good-looking woman over there. Singing? Not singing." When his shoelaces come untied, I kneel before his dazzling *New Balance* sneakers. "Thank you," he says wholeheartedly. "You're my kind of woman."

Mother and I accompany him on the nature trail. Dad leads the way single file, walking so slowly that I suffer from the illusion I'm moving backward, as if my train were being passed on the next track by a flatcar carrying vegetation. He stumbles several times. I think of how he used to bound ahead. The change makes me despondent, but I don't feel I've lost him. In fact, I'm more a daughter than ever before, and, in some profound way, he is more my father. Turning to smile at Mother and me, he jokes, "I have to look back to see if the girls are still there."

Yes, they are.

During an appointment for Dad's monthly B-12 shot, the physician's assistant tells Mother that Dad's swallowing problem is very serious, warning that he could develop pneumonia from material aspirated into his lungs. He's scheduled to go to the hospital for a procedure that involves putting a tube down his throat to look around and possibly widen his esophagus, if needed. Mother can't give me a lot of details on the phone, except to say he'll need some sort of anesthesia.

I'm appalled. Everything I've heard and read emphasizes that anesthesia throws Alzheimer's patients into irreversible confusion. When I mention this to Mother, she says they can do the procedure without anesthesia, but Dad could never tolerate it.

"Pneumonia's not the worst way to go," I hazard.

"I don't want him to starve to death!" she says, raising her voice.

"Don't you think he can get along for a while with nutritional drinks?"

"Then his stomach will shrink," she objects, moving on to say she's had to fill out a long questionnaire—on the bottom, she's written that she wants to stay with him until the anesthesia takes effect. "Now, don't *you* get upset."

Next morning, she calls again. "I've made a decision," she says. "This morning, I went over to the hospital and told them I was canceling. After observing your father, I've decided that the problem is not his swallowing, but the way he stuffs food in his mouth. No one could swallow what he puts in his mouth."

"I'm very relieved," I manage to get out.

"I'm going to be much more careful about what I feed him," she says. "He does fine with cereals and soups."

"Of course, it's possible that the reason his mouth is full of food is because he can't swallow." I don't know why I'm saying this.

"I don't think so," she says. "You've seen how fast he eats."

Mother, with you in charge, there's little to do but write. First draft and revisions, I'm given chances to respond with more insight. Writing reduces the agony of the spectator, forced, as I am, to stand back and watch Dad choke on too much forgetting. I know you think it's terrible that inside sources have revealed details of President Reagan's decline to the tabloids. I'm sorry I've betrayed you and Dad in this matter, once by considering pneumonia, and again by writing about it.

September *10*, Dad's eighty-sixth birthday. Dad spots the pile of cards and gifts and wonders, "Who are they for?" "You, Dad! Happy Birthday!" Seated next to Mother on the sofa, he proceeds to open everything with humility. The two gifts David and I chose go over well—a knit shirt decorated with the Ocean Park logo, and a freestyle puzzle made by LEGO, advertising *A Different Puzzle Every Time! 25 double sided interchangeable pieces. Ages 3 and up.* On the card, I've written, "You can't go wrong!"

"I'm sort of overwhelmed by this whole thing," Dad says.

Loring and Lindy come over for ice cream and apple crisp, made from apples I picked yesterday in New Hampshire. It's my idea to serve apple crisp, thinking Dad might be able to swallow it more easily than cake. Mother puts a candle on his portion, and we sing "Happy Birthday." It's such a pleasure to be with friends who knew Dad before and are comfortable with him now, remaining unperturbed when he sits in a rocker and pulls his knees toward his chest, as if a vacuum cleaner probed around his feet. At their departure, Dad transforms into a host, graciously thanking them for coming.

In the evening, he and I sit in front of the national news. He's overstimulated, restless, and chatty. I'm trying to hear about the Starr Report. "You're a darned good driver! If I were your father, I'd be proud of you," he states.

I've spent the whole day with him. Can't I have a minute's peace?

"You mean the world to me," he says in an undertone, as I crane impatiently to catch what Peter Jennings is saying. "You mean the world to me," he rehearses. Just as I'm about to storm out, he rises and goes through the dining room to the kitchen doorway. "You mean the world to me, Katherine," he says to Mother.

After she joins us in the living room, I escape to the dark porch. I'm so tense, the tears have trouble fighting their way out of my eyes. Mother comes to see what I'm doing. "Are you upset?" she asks from the door.

My try at a reply in a normal voice collapses. "It's so hard," I sob, as she comes around behind me and strokes my forehead. "It's so hard."

"I know," she soothes. "I know."

I climb the stairs to rest in the bedroom. Below me, Dad is napping noisily in the den. Songs and monologues drift up through the floorboards, subsiding at intervals into groans and sighs on the exhale. I experiment with a few satisfying groans of my own. A macabre chorus, we lie stacked one above the other like bodies in a vault, he the lead singer, I the backup, trying to synchronize my groans with his.

*D*ad's sister, Miriam, has died. Mother quietly delivers the news on the porch. Aware of the gravity of the moment, he looks down, gathers himself, and says, "Well, it was inevitable." Pausing, he resumes, "I'm not surprised to hear this. It's a relief, really. She was in that place a long time."

Mother murmurs agreement. He continues, "Miriam was a lot of fun. We had some good times together." Assent all around.

He looks up, signaling the close of his remarks. "It will happen to all of us someday."

Mother and I regretfully concur.

"Someday, I'll be dead," he concludes.

He and I walk to get the paper. "Where were you born?" he asks on the way back.

"Montpelier, Vermont."

"For heaven's sake! I was up there for a while, you know. I miss New Hampshire. My birthplace! September *10, 1912.* That makes me eighty-six. I don't feel that old," he says, adding with a chuckle, "Some things I don't forget."

On the phone Mother comments, "This Sunday is our fifty-seventh wedding anniversary."

"Yes!" I exclaim.

"I'm not going to tell your father. He won't get it. The other night, he said, 'Now where do I sleep tonight?' When I showed him the bedroom, he claimed he'd never been in there before."

"That *is* surprising. I suppose you could make a joke of it."

"Oh, no. I would never tease him about something like that."

"I hope you aren't going to feel too bad," I venture.

"No," she says. "I've just been thinking about how much we have to be thankful for."

Mother is so brave. You know you are hearing a cry from a wounded heart, when someone says, "I have much to be thankful for."

"*C*'est la vie," Dad reads from a sign over a garage on their street.

"Je ne sais de quoi," I respond, ransacking my high school French.

"Oui, Madame, c'est bon," he shoots back.

I park at Bass Hole, and we take our customary walk to the end of the bridge. Across the creek, the dunes are deserted. As we retrace our steps, a stranger approaches. "They're waiting for you back there," Dad calls out. The man gives a cordial laugh.

"I like you. You've got a good sense of humor," Dad says, patting him on the upper arm.

After lunch, David and I offer to help Dad buy his Christmas gift for Mother, an address book she's had her eye on. When told the plan, he acts bewildered, even frightened. "Nancy knows what to do," Mother reassures him. At CVS, we talk ourselves through the process, confounded by racks of address books so subtly dissimilar that only the address books themselves could recognize their own kind. Safely home, David wraps, and Dad helps with the tape, choosing a drawer in the den for the hiding place. "Is today the day?" he asks hopefully, his open face its most shining.

Late afternoon, Dad and I take a walk to the neighborhood beyond the playground, where new houses rise from the sandy dirt. A north wind pushes us, gusting into our faces as we circle past a yapping sheltie patrolling its property. Dad pulls me close. Arms linked, we force our way along like two sailboats in heavy seas, or one boat with two sails.

*M*other discovers an error on her credit card bill, a forty-nine-dollar unauthorized charge for a credit report. I offer to call and try to straighten the matter out. Perched on a stool in my bathrobe, I negotiate with various representatives, while Mother hands me documents, and Dad fusses in the coat closet, anxious to get the paper.

"Gilbert! It's raining! Nancy will drive you up when she gets off the phone!"

He feints like a quarterback and lunges again toward the coats. Deflected, he retreats to the kitchen to get two quarters to pay for the paper. Back in the closet, he mutters, "It's not raining."

"Yes, it is," Mother insists. "You have to wait."

I'm having trouble hearing. "Take him to the porch and show him the rain," I hiss to Mother. "I'm sorry," I apologize to the woman on the other end of the line. Finally, I get off the phone. What used to be miserable suddenly becomes unbearable. I throw on some clothes and hurry outside with Dad. The last grains of patience rush through the hourglass. "You see? It *is* raining!" I snap. In the car, Dad says, "Your mother's upset about something. I don't know what." Errand accomplished, we follow Mother's instructions, draping our rain-soaked jackets over chairs, instead of on hangers in the closet, where everything is dry. Dad works on his crossword puzzle. I lie on the sofa, with my eyes closed.

On the drive to New Hampshire through rain and snow, a rock off a construction vehicle gouges my windshield. Gripping the steering wheel, my arms relive the good-bye hugs. I never know which parent to hug first. At home in my rocking chair, I'm hypnotized by three sofa pillows patterned in zigzags. Sinking further, I become a planet endangered by streaking comets with serious faces, my mother and father, my sisters, my husband and sons. Hunched and alone, I feel what anchors must feel deep below the surface, pinned by their own weight to the sea floor, responsible for the chains, and for the ships flying like kites in another world.

"How was your Christmas?" I ask Mother on the phone.

"We didn't have a very good start," she says. "Your father paid no attention to the gifts I'd arranged in the living room. All he wanted to do was go outside and shovel a path for the mailman."

"Could he open his presents himself?"

"Pretty much. He thought the apron you gave him was to wear bowling." Mother had said he needed a new apron, so I'd ordered an apron for each of them, embroidered with their names and a little design—for her, a white rose, for him, a red bowling ball knocking over white pins.

"Have you had a chance to listen to the Perry Como tapes?"

"Yes! I've played the religious one several times."

Before wrapping the Perry Como tapes, I'd listened to them both, one his top hits, like "Hot Diggity Dog" and "Catch a Falling Star," and the other a mix ranging from "I Believe" and "Scarlet Ribbons" to "When You Come to the End of the Day." On his weekly TV show, Perry projected the image of a family man, relaxed and a bit melancholy. Forty years later, his music still resonates, though muted, as if each song had hatched like a butterfly, fluttered about, and been stuffed back in its cocoon. Bombarded by dreams, we basked in the black and white light of the 1950s, unaware that a smile is a vessel curved to hold sorrow.

Dad's dreams have gained strength, like nobles who band together. He woke at 4:00 A.M. convinced somebody was waiting for him, and he had to get in touch so they wouldn't worry. Mother held him in her arms.

Calmer, he said, "You're a nice person. What's your name?"

"Katherine."

"The same name as my wife!" he remarked.

They slept. At breakfast, Dad craned his neck. "Where is she?" he asked. He was looking for the lady from last night.

"Don't go near the top of the stairs with him, if he's like that again," I warn on the phone. "Our neighbor had Alzheimer's and wandered the house at night. Her husband went looking for her, and she pushed him down the stairs. She was bigger than he was."

"Your father's never been violent with me."

"She didn't realize he was her husband. She thought he was a burglar."

In his heart, Dad recognizes Mother. Perhaps this is the way we know God. We look straight at God and ask, *Where are You?* We are held. Our names fall away, like the toys a child sleeps with. Nameless, yet recognized—perhaps this is the way God knows us.

February. I arrive at 8:00 P.M. Dad's already in his pajamas. Coming into the kitchen, he tries to shake my hand. "Hi, Dad," I say, crushing him in a hug. After he goes to bed, Mother fills me in on the latest news. Before breakfast the other morning, he said to her, "Where is the person who takes care of me?" Another time, they were loading bags of groceries from the shopping cart into the car. When Mother closed the trunk, she found Dad trying to get into a sport utility vehicle parked next to their Honda Accord. In Macy's, she went down the escalator and realized at the bottom that he wasn't with her. "Fortunately, he was able to get on by himself. From now on, I'll take him by the arm," she says. "Lately, there's been a lot of little surprises."

Next morning, she does errands in the car. Dad settles at the kitchen table with the crossword and then joins me in the living room. "When I was a lifeguard at Ocean Park, I saved some lives," he comments.

"Uh-huh." I'm stretched out on the sofa, absorbed in the paper.

He totters to his feet and wanders off. I switch to Mother's chair. Having sunk into my customary lethargy, changing chairs is a recordable event. Dad comes back into the room, without anything to do. I burst into song—

> If you go down in the woods today,
> you're sure of a big surprise.
> If you go down in the woods today,
> you'd better go in disguise.
> For every bear that ever there was
> will gather there for certain, because
> today's the day the teddy bears have their picnic.

Delighted, Dad stands with his mouth open. Cocking his head and holding one finger up, he hurries into the kitchen, returns promptly, and hands me a dollar.

I invite him for a walk past the playground. Mother has cautioned me to come back the short way—he tires easily. Dad remembers our last excursion here, when the wind blew so strongly and the dog barked. No sign of the dog today. "It's a good thing I'm married," he says roguishly, "or I'd be after you." At the end of the street, he asks, "Do you want to go left or right?"

"Left."

"Good," he says with a twinkle in his eye. "That's what I would have said. If you'd said 'right,' I'd have said, 'Are you sure that's what you want?'"

"I don't know what I'm going to do, when you leave," Dad says, miming a sad face. Ever since my arrival, he's harped on various aspects of my departure.

"I don't know what I'm going to do, when you leave," he repeats. I barely look at him. "Because I love you," he adds.

"I love you, too," I say firmly. I wish I'd said it first. We should toss the words around more often, perfecting our throw, so that they sink into the heart's glove like a baseball caught right.

After lunch, he heads upstairs for a nap. "Why don't you say good-bye to him now," Mother advises.

"Let's play it by ear," I say, hoping he won't nap for long. I'm not ready to say good-bye.

Half an hour later, I load the car, climb the stairs, ease open the bedroom door, and tiptoe across the room. He's fast asleep on his side, the blanket pulled over his nose. All I can see are wisps of white hair and his forehead freckled with age. I kiss two of my fingers, send the kiss into the air above his shoulder, and creep away.

Downstairs, Mother and I share a long embrace. "I couldn't bring myself to wake him." I shrug helplessly.

"That's all right," she says. "He'll understand."

I start the car. "Do you think he's awake yet?" I call.

She goes into the house to listen at the bottom of the stairs. "Not yet," she answers in an undertone.

Sunday, March *14, 1999*. Dad falls in the living room. Mother finds him lying against the sofa near the bookcase and calls *911*. Within minutes, they arrive, support him in a walking position, and put him on a stretcher in the driveway. Mother follows the ambulance to the hospital, where they spend four hours in the emergency room. Mother can see the line on the heart monitor jumping around. Late in the day, after he seems to have calmed down, they ask him to walk prior to releasing him. The nurse says, *Stop.* The heart monitor is going crazy again. He's admitted to the hospital, and eventually Mother goes home.

Next day, she returns to the hospital around lunch time and spends a harrowing afternoon intercepting his moves, pressing his chest down, and holding his hands, to prevent him from pulling out his IV needle and catheter. At four o'clock, a competent matron comes on duty, tells her to go home, and ties Dad's arms to the bed. Mother's ready to obey. She assures me she doesn't want me to come down yet. Dad's slated to be moved to the Manor, an extended care community. A representative will determine how he could benefit from their program. Dad's not able to walk, whether because of his heart, sedation, or something else, we don't know. One of the nurses asked if he'd ever used a walker. They don't realize that just last week he could walk to the new neighborhood beyond the playground. I wish they could see him do the frogstand.

"How are *you* doing?" I ask.

"I'm all right. The worst part was coming home to an empty house for the first time."

"That must have been traumatic."

"It was, but I'm getting used to it."

106

"I'm upset to hear that his arms are tied down."

"They're not really tied down. They're sort of on tethers. He can move them around. He doesn't like the catheter. He'd tear it out if he could." She goes on to tell me about the man in the bed next to Dad. He has Alzheimer's, too, and broke his arm. No one has visited him. "We've been lucky," she says with pity.

When David and I enter the house the following Saturday, no one shows us an album or old postcard. Conversation is possible. I feel extremely ambivalent about these changes. Mother can't get used to being able to put something down, without it disappearing. The doctor thinks a temporary heart fibrillation caused Dad's collapse. From the disarray on the bookshelves, she's deduced that he was probably reaching for the picture of his mother and father. He's been in the Manor since yesterday, in a room with two roommates. "Today, he walked with a walker that was too small," she says. "The nurses are looking for a taller one. There's a common room with big windows and a white bird in a cage."

Next to the phone, I spot a piece of scrap paper covered with notes Mother has written to herself—in the center, in Dad's handwriting, are the words,

Katherine
(I love her!)

"You'd better save this," I urge. "It might be the last thing he ever wrote." I attach it to the front of the refrigerator under a magnet.

"He says that to me every day!"

We drive to Bass Hole to walk on the bridge and visit the new platform overlooking the salt marsh. Mother murmurs, "This is the first time I've walked without your father."

"It's hard to do things without him that we did so often with him." I sound like a self-help manual.

"It's an adjustment to a new time of life," she comments bleakly.

Our attention is caught by a white gull dropping an object onto the sand from twenty feet up. "He's breaking open razor clams," David reports from a closer vantage point. While we watch, another gull releases a shell, flies down, and feasts.

Over a supper of pork, beans, sweet roll, and coleslaw, Mother muses, "I wonder if they're helping him eat."

"If you want, David and I could visit at times when you're not usually there, to see how they're taking care of him."

"No, I wouldn't spy on them."

"Is he having more trouble eating?"

"He's not eating well. He doesn't swallow. They asked me what kinds of foods he likes, and I told them he should be on foods that are easy to swallow. He can drink all right. He won't be able to gain his strength back, if he can't eat."

Sunday morning, David and I drive with apprehension to the Manor. Mother will join us later, to help with lunch. According to her directions, we're to go in the front door, turn right, and look for the desk. Dad's room is three doors down. As we walk along the corridor, David says, "There he is." Dad is positioned close to the desk, restrained behind a tray in an upholstered chair on wheels. Struggling to escape, he hears David's voice, looks up, and sees us. His mouth drops open. I rush forward, gathering him in my arms as best I can, kissing his forehead, laughing, hugging, patting, repeating, "Dad, Dad, it's Nancy and David." A smiling nurse approaches and suggests we wheel Dad into the common room. I push, while David scouts up a free table. Dad says he's thirsty, so David goes to get him a cup of water. Dad is completely overcome. "I couldn't believe my eyes when you came in," he says. "I thought I was seeing things. Are you here to take me home?"

My heart thuds. I speak into his ear. "You've had a fall, Dad. You need to stay here and practice walking." David returns with water and a box of tissues. Dad takes a sip. "Do you know what kind of a place this is? It could be a campus in the state system," he surmises.

"It's called the Manor," I answer evasively and change the subject. "You look good." He's wearing corduroys and a green plaid shirt Gail made him years ago.

"I do?" he replies, flattered. "When I saw you and David, I almost fell over. It's the last thing I expected to see." His eyes mist. "Maybe I'm not going to die. How did you know where I was?"

"Mother told us," we explain.

"How did she know?"

"Mother knows where you are," we assure him. "She'll be here soon."

"She will?" He raises his eyebrows. "You and David are two of the finest people in the world."

"At last, the recognition we deserve."

He goes on, "'Who's that good-looking guy?' I said to myself. 'It's David!'"

"I'm good-looking, too. David's not the only one."

"Of course you are." His face clouds over. "How did you find me?" I take out the map Mother drew and spread it on his tray. With a pencil, I trace the route. "Here we are, right here," I point, drawing a star and *DAD* next to the road. Looking sideways at me, his lower lip trembles, and his eyes fill. "I love you," he says.

"I love you, too," I reply, swinging my head to show off my new earrings worn especially for him, made from the keys of an antique typewriter. One shows $ over 4, and the other (over 9. "Aren't those great!" he says.

After lunch at the mall, David and I return to find Mother and Dad at a table in the common room, accompanied by Loring and Lindy. Dad presides over the assemblage in his new tall walker. Free of that cramped chair and tray, he beams from his perch and joins in the conversation. Mother tells us in an aside that his lunch was pureed, and he ate better.

A physical therapist approaches and says it's time for Dad's therapy session. "Would you like to walk with me?" she asks Dad. He doesn't comprehend. "It's time to practice walking," we tell him. I turn his walker, and we encourage him to stand. "Like this?" he asks. "Yes, good!" He takes an uncertain step. "Come along," the therapist beckons. "I'd follow you to the ends of the earth," Dad says to her.

*T*he slope has turned steep. Dad spent a couple of weeks in rehab at the Manor. They were kind to him, but he kept asking to go home. Mother wanted him home, too. She had more success than the nurses in getting him to take a few teaspoons of soft food. April 1, she brought him home. Two days later, I got a call. "I think I'm going to need you," she said in a strained voice. I raced down, to find Dad in his recliner, his cardigan wrapped around his shoulders. Rug stains testified to apple juice he spit out. Early evening, with great difficulty, we put him to bed, supporting him on either side. The next day was Easter Sunday. We managed to get him back in his recliner, nearly falling in a heap over the cat lounging in the doorway. In the afternoon, we watched Fred Astaire and Judy Garland sing and dance in *Easter Parade.* When bedtime rolled around again, Dad clenched up on top of the covers, as if in pain. Since he couldn't tell us what was wrong, we had no choice but to call the ambulance. It turns out he was suffering from urinary retention, possibly caused by a blockage, medication, or changes in the brain. Once in the hospital, things went from bad to worse. He was drugged, underwent a diagnostic procedure, and one night escaped his bed and fell in the corridor. "Your father has acted very inappropriately," a nurse said in a tone of reproof. I was speechless. She seemed to know nothing about dementia. Having ruled out a blockage, the hospital discharged him back to the Manor, to the very same bed he left the week before.

Mother and I arrive at the Manor late in the morning, after he's been settled in. As we drive to the parking area, I caution, "He might be the worst we've ever seen him." We find him lying in bed, eyes closed, face drawn. Mother takes the chair next to him and puts her hand on his arm. I stand behind her. "Gil," she says softly. "We're here."

He opens his eyes, sees us, and smiles. Looking at Mother, he says, "Beauty and the beast, and you're the beauty." She smiles back at him. My throat tightens. "I'm going to take a walk." Mother nods, her eyes fixed on Dad.

I escape through the front door, holding back sobs until out of view of the picture window. Circling the brick building, I compose myself and return to Dad's bedside. Mother cedes her place. I pat his arm, exclaiming, "You're back in your own room!"

Turning his head on the pillow, he notices my Key West rooster T-shirt. "Cock-a-doodle-doo," I crow. I'm deliriously happy that he survived the hospital.

Dad laughs. "Beauty and the beast ... " he starts to say.

"And you're the beauty!" I jump in, stealing his line.

"No," he says and grins.

Next day, I spell Mother in the afternoon. Dad's in bed. Earlier, he and Mother took a wheelchair jaunt to the common room. He looks at his watch. "It's 2:05," he announces. "I want to get up." Surprised, I check my own watch. He's right.

I find a nurse. "He needs a quiet time now," she says, "but we can sit him straighter. I'll show you how to do that."

I crank Dad up, making a game of it. He isn't amused. The nurse leaves.

"I feel kind of hopeless," he says quietly. Overwhelmed, I say nothing.

"I feel kind of helpless," he continues, after a pause. This is something I can tackle. "That's because you're so weak," I explain. "The people here are going to help you get your strength back. There are some very nice people here."

"Yes, I've seen them walking back and forth," he says, nodding toward the corridor. A loud woman not in possession of her senses is shuffling past. He seems bored. "You could watch TV," I suggest. On the animal channel, a vet is holding open a husky's mouth, demonstrating how to brush a dog's teeth.

"I'm not facing that way," Dad says feebly.

I start to sing "The Old Rugged Cross" and move into "Are Ye Able," doing a clumsy job with both. Dad calms down. I rack my brains, unable to come up with another hymn. I slog through "The Old Mill Stream." So many songs I could sing to him, but my mind is blank. Coming to my aid, Dad says, "What will you be doing next, when you go home?"

"Not too much," I reply. I plan to drive home tomorrow, with the understanding that I'll come back at a moment's notice.

Like a foot soldier come off night watch, Dad sleeps.

For the thing which I greatly feared
is come upon me, and that which I was
afraid of is come unto me.
—The Book of Job 3:25

I am navigating Dad's wheelchair down a corridor crowded with pedestrians and other wheelchairs propelled by crazy drivers. Dad has to hold his feet off the floor, because this chair has no footrest. Stuck behind a woman about four feet tall who doesn't seem to care that she's blocking traffic, I feel the stirrings of road rage. Eventually, we make it to the common room, and I steer over to the birdcage. "Look at the white bird in there," I say, directing Dad's attention to the beleaguered occupant. A pallid woman sits on a couch next to the cage, communing with the bird. I hate to disturb her. Dad looks mildly pleased. "My car is out there," I announce, pushing him toward the front windows.

"Oh?" Cars still interest him. In the center of the room, people have formed a circle around a woman with wild white hair and the air of a games mistress. A blue rubber ball the size of a beach ball bounces back and forth among those gathered, although some seem reluctant.

"Don't send it to me," one woman screeches. The ball comes careening her way, and she ducks. Whenever the ball goes astray, the leader retrieves it and, with a mighty bounce, directs it back into the circle.

Dad watches for a moment with a smile on his face. There was a time when he would have scoffed at such goings-on. I look for a free table, where we can have a talk, but all are taken. Slowly, we head back to the nurses' station. I say to a nurse, "I'm going to have to leave soon. Where would you like me to put Dad?"

"You can leave him right here, where we'll keep an eye on him," she says.

I push him over next to the opposite wall. Well, this is it. I'm going to have to say good-bye in the corridor. Leaning forward in a half-crouch, I say urgently, "Dad, listen. Let go of your sadness. Let God's love into your heart." He seems to be taking in my words. In case he feels hopeless again, I continue, "Remember God's love. Remember Jesus. God is with you." I'm running out of religious counsel. He looks bemused. "Give me a kiss," I say, holding his face. I kiss him on the lips, and, as I do, he kisses me. A light kiss good-bye. I grope my way toward the exit. Turning, I realize I've left him facing away, sparing our eyes a direct look.

Over the next ten days, Andrea and Gail make their way to the Manor. I'm in New Hampshire, lending support from a distance.

"Dad's had another bad day," Mother reports, her throat raspy. "It goes up and down. Yesterday, he surprised me. We were in the common room, and he looked around and said distinctly, *There are fewer people in this room than at any time since I've been here.*"

"How are you holding up?" I ask. It's understood that she wants to go through this alone with Dad.

"Oh, you know." She takes a long breath. "Today, I was sitting next to his bed, stroking him. I told him I loved him, and he said, *Sweetheart.*"

At dusk, I walk along Mink Brook, through field grass crushed by winter's nets. The air shimmers pink and gray, as though, after a long day, the colors finally can relax. I think of Dad in his room, in the corner away from the window. It hits me that he may never see the sky again. Weeping, I make my way home, imagining a sun nearly eclipsed, sending out a spray of light, like a black dog shaking his coat, bathing us with countless, infinitesimal drops.

*T*hursday, April 22. Unquiet, not knowing when a call might come, I decide to pay a visit to our local science museum, which has advertised that baby snakes are on view during school vacation week. Never having seen a baby snake in person, I think it might take my mind off things.

I arrive at the museum, pay the hefty admission price, get my hand stamped, and head upstairs, past bubble tanks, panoramas of forest and grassland, kinetic sculptures, a beehive, and a large colony of leaf cutter ants hastening along Plexiglas tubing. Children and parents swarm throughout the complex. According to a sign, a snake show is scheduled shortly. *My good luck!* Reaching the glass case where the snakes reside, I peer in. Two adult boa constrictors, named Victoria and Al, slumber in a tangle. The case isn't big enough for them to stretch out, if boas ever stretch out. I can't see any sign of the babies.

"They're in there," a white-haired volunteer in a smock assures me.

My eyes follow the curves, to no avail. Other curiosity-seekers crowd in, and I crane over their shoulders, hoping for the rivers of snake to part. "Here comes Nancy," the volunteer calls out. "Everyone back, please." I'm always startled at the sound of my name. A second woman in a smock bustles forward, opens the case, chooses a snake, lifts it with two hands, and drapes it around her neck. As soon as she's moved off toward the exhibition site, the crowd surges against the case, to see the babies.

"The babies aren't there," Nancy informs us, her hands caressing her scaly stole.

"Where are they?" I ask.

"They've been taken to the basement, to see if they'll eat."

Although everyone else follows her for the show, I turn away, disappointed. Even the tiny children seem to be taking this better than I am. Passing the leaf cutter ants, I pause to observe their toils through a magnifying lens, but blatant industry worsens my mood. At the admission desk, I say plaintively, "The baby snakes aren't upstairs. They're in the basement somewhere. I've come all the way just to see them." I don't mention that 'all the way' is a two-mile drive from New Hampshire, across the Connecticut River to Vermont.

The employee who took my money and stamped my hand can see I'm upset. Perhaps she intuits that my upset goes far beyond baby snakes. At any rate, she takes pity on me. "I know where they are," she says helpfully. "Follow me." She leads me to a metal door that opens on the service area. A few feet inside, a small cage rests on the floor, covered by burlap and lit by a heat lamp. She lifts the burlap, tucks it up, and gestures me closer. "They're in here," she says in a low voice. "You can observe them. I have to get back." She vanishes, leaving me unsupervised.

I crouch down. Behind the smudged glass, two baby boa constrictors coexist in a red glow. One of them is motionless. The other grips a hairless baby mouse head first in its yawning jaws. As I watch, gagging, the snake flexes its throat muscles around its unprotesting prey. A lump travels to the sinuous midsection and stops. I rock back on my heels, seesawing between fascination and horror. Not only baby snakes, but baby snakes eating, I enter in my mental catalogue of firsts. Deciding I've had enough, I glance in the cage prior to rising to my feet. *Oh, no.* I can't tear my eyes away. The snake has spotted another fetal comma curled inertly on the cage floor. "Aren't you going to leave something for someone else?" I coax. Grabbed by its tail, this mouse, more vocal, utters squeals of terror, before taking its place next to the first.

I stagger to my feet. The heat lamp shuts off, plunging the cage in darkness. I lower the burlap and open the metal door. Pushing and pulling, my emotions propel me along, many hands supporting one banner. Dazed, I thank the lady at the desk. "I saw one of the babies eat two mice," I say faintly. "This must be your lucky day!" she says. "If you want to look at it that way," I reply, and make my way out to the parking lot, bent over, arms so full of troubles I'm forced to carry enjoyment on my back. In the car on the way home, I mutter, "This is nature. Life and death. The grand design."

On my return, the machine displays one message. I steel myself. Mother's voice, filled with grief, spills into the room: *Hi, Nancy. Dad died at one o'clock. Will you call me back as soon as you come in?* Unused to leaving messages, she pauses, and, to signal the end of the transmission, tosses a shaky final word into the machine—*Okay.*

━✗

*M*other had prayed she would be with Dad when he died. At his side in the morning, she continued her vigil, murmuring words of love and stroking his head. His breathing quickened in response. She felt he knew she was there. She kissed him and said, "It's okay to go now." At one o'clock, his face became alert, as though he saw someone he knew. He closed his mouth, took three breaths through his nose, exhaled, and was still.

That evening, after David and I arrived, we three sat in the living room and talked a little. I took Dad's recliner.

"I wondered if I'd be able to remember him the way he used to be. Immediately, I remembered," Mother said in an exhausted, numb voice. "All this business has evaporated away. I remember him the way he was."

At the end of May, after a memorial service, the family scattered Dad's ashes over water, with one handful kept back for the small-leaf rhododendron, which was blooming on the day he died.

I look at death
as though across a body of water,
the opposite shore closer
with the passing of every year.
One day, I will step across
and turn back for a moment,
the way I glance up from a book
at the sound of a branch brushing
against the window.

Life and death are a couple long married,
finding evidence of one another
in everything familiar,
so bound together in service
that parted, they are lost.
I look across a body of water,
gaze unfocused.
If asked, I could not say
what I have seen.

Sources

Coleridge, Samuel Taylor. *The Rime of the Ancient Mariner.* New York: The Heritage Club, *1938.*

Greenberg, Martin H. & Ed Gorman, eds. *Cat Crimes II.* Thorndike, Maine: G.K. Hall & Co., *1992.*

Hanh, Thich Nhat. *The Miracle of Mindfulness.* Boston: Beacon Press, *1975.*

"I Love You Truly." Words and music by Carrie Jacobs-Bond.

Kenyon, Jim. "'It's Like He Stepped Out The Door And Vanished.'" *Valley News.* Volume *46:* No. *67.* August *14, 1997.*

Lederer, Richard. *Anguished English.* New York: Dell Publishing, *1987.*

Milton, John. *Complete Poetry & Selected Prose.* New York: The Modern Library, *1950.*

Mitchell, Stephen, ed. and trans. "The Sonnets to Orpheus II, *13.*" *The Selected Poetry of Rainer Maria Rilke.* New York: Vintage International, *1989.*

Pinsky, Robert, trans. T*he Inferno of Dante.* New York: Farrar, Straus and Giroux, *1994.*

"The Teddy Bears' Picnic." Words and music by John W. Bratton and James B. Kennedy. ©*1907* (Renewed) Warner Bros. Inc. All rights reserved. Used by permission of Warner Bros. Publications U.S. Inc., Miami, Florida..

The Marie Alexander Poetry Series

Series Editor: Robert Alexander

Volume 8
Light From An Eclipse
Nancy Lagomarsino

Volume 7
A Handbook for Writers
Vern Rutsala

Volume 6
The Blue Dress
Alison Townsend

Volume 5
Moments Without Names:
New & Selected Prose Poems
Morton Marcus

Volume 4
Whatever Shines
Kathleen McGookey

Volume 3
Northern Latitudes
Lawrence Millman

Volume 2
Your Sun, Manny
Marie Harris

Volume I
Traffic
Jack Anderson